Canadians and War
Volume 3

Edited by Jeremy Lammi
Introduction by Jeremy Lammi

Essays by
Dr. Lisa M. Daly
Melissa Hermes
Keith Donaldson
Amanda Shepherd
W. A. Leavey

Lammi
Publishing Inc.

Published by Lammi Publishing, Inc. Headquartered in Coaldale, Alberta, Canada. http:// lammipublishing.ca

Cover Image Credits
Gilbert Alexander Milne/Canada. Dept. of National Defence/Library and Archives Canada/PA-122765
Lieut. Frederick G. Whitcombe / Canada. Dept. of National Defence / Library and Archives Canada / PA-163411

Text and content editing by Karen Hann.
Cover design by Paul Hewitt Battlefield Design, UK. Book layout by www.ebooklaunch.com

Table of Contents

Introduction
by Jeremy Lammi

It has been over two centuries since Canada, first as a British colony and then as a Dominion, has fought an international conflict within its own borders. Few other nations can say the same. Yet, we have been steadily involved in military conflicts for most of our history. In the third edition of Canadians and War, we are reminded of how far the reach of war has been.

War does not only exist on the battlefield. It exists in the training grounds; it exists in the parliamentary and congressional halls and countless offices and meeting spaces; it exists in the endless spaces and routes of support and supply over land, air, and sea; it exists in the collective psyche of nations dedicating endless resources to the home front effort and sending their strongest and bravest to potential slaughter; it exists in the textbooks and the memoires; and it exists in the minds and souls of those whose injuries are not visible to the naked eye. This third edition of *Canadians and War* gives a small glimpse of the vastness of this reach.

Not all Canadian soldiers were from Canada. We examine the home front in the First World War from a surprising location in Melissa Hermes's "They Fought for King and Country: Otter Tail County Men in the CEF." Beyond the battlefield, we get a sense of the massive support and supply system for the Canadian Forces in the Second World War, as well as how that system affected some very famous people and built Canadian communities, in Dr. Lisa M. Daly's "Sacrifice in Second World War Gander: The Death of Sir Frederick Banting and the First Canadians Buried in the Commonwealth War Graves." This piece recounts some of the more dramatic and tragic moments of the early years of that small, but strategically and commercially vital Gander airstrip. From Keith Donaldson, we experience WW2 Italian battlefields in "Breaching the Gustav Line: The 1st Canadian Armoured Brigade and the 8th Indian Division, May 1944," learning how regiments from two nations on opposite sides of the globe came together to achieve a vital, but little-known military objective. Donaldson teaches us how, the Canadian tankers in support of the 8th Indian Division helped pave the way for the ultimate Allied drive to Rome. Moving beyond fixed spaces in time, we explore how war is experienced in memory in Amanda Shepherd's "We Survived by Luck, God, Fate and Training: Army Memoires of the Second World War." This piece discusses not only the memoires themselves, but also how war memoires can be studied as historical documents. Our final journey takes us into the human mind itself and scrutinizes the devastating effect military life can have on the psyche in Lieutenant-Colonel (ret'd) W. A. Leavey's treatise on operational stress injuries: "Leadership and OSIs in the Canadian Army." Leavey draws not only on medical and historical sources, but also on his many years of military service to offer an extensive picture of OSIs and how effective military leadership is a crucial tool in recognizing, handling, and mitigating those wounds of the mind.

We are very pleased that you're about to take this journey with us.

List of Contributors

Dr. Lisa M. Daly

Dr. Lisa M. Daly has been researching the aviation history of Newfoundland and Labrador, Canada, and archaeologically investigating the remains of aircraft that crashed and still litter the landscape of the province. Her doctorate from Memorial University of Newfoundland focused on the airbase in Gander, but her work has taken her around the island and as far as Goose Bay. Her overall focus has been early aviation in Newfoundland and Labrador, from the Great Atlantic Air Race to the immediate post-World War II period, but she has done contract work for sites as recent as 1978. Recently she started working as an archaeologist for the province of New Brunswick, but she is continuing to research and promote her home province's aviation history. Her research can be followed at www.planecrashgirl.ca

Keith Donaldson

Keith Donaldson completed his bachelor's degree in history at Simon Fraser University in 2005, and his Masters degree in History at the University of Calgary in 2008. He teaches Social Studies, History, and French at the secondary level in Metro Vancouver, British Columbia with a particular passion for Canada's military history and heritage. This article is Keith's first publication, and draws heavily on research conducted for his master's thesis.

W. A. Leavey

Lieutenant-Colonel (Retired) W.A. (Bill) Leavey served in the Canadian Army Infantry from 1967 to 2008. The field units he served in include the Black Watch, Royal Highland Regiment of Canada (RHC), the Royal Canadian Regiment (RCR), the Canadian Airborne Regiment (CAR), and the Princess of Wales Own Regiment (PWOR). From 1994 to 1998 he was seconded with Veterans Affairs Canada as military liaison officer for the Canada Remembers Program, a commemoration group celebrating battle and campaign anniversaries for all of Canada's major wartime events. LCol Leavey holds a master's degree in English from the Royal Military College. He has written two books of anecdotes for the RHC and RCR, entitled War Stories, Anecdotes and Lies. LCol Leavey has also published numerous stories, articles, and essays on military humour and humour in general in local and national magazines and newspapers. In the past two years Leavey has written Essays for both Volume 1 and 2 of Military History. He lives in Kingston, Ontario with his wife Maureen, a 35-year veteran herself, and their mini-Australian Labradoodle (part Kangaroo), Finnigan

Amanda Shepherd

Amanda Shepherd has just successfully graduated with her Master of Arts degree from the University of New Brunswick in Canadian Military History. She comes from a long line of military members and plans to continue her research into her family's involvement in the World Wars and Afghan War. She has presented her research at several conferences across Canada and made presentations about remembrance in her hometown of Saint John, New Brunswick. Amanda cannot wait to visit the Canadian battlefields in Europe again to advance her knowledge on the topic. She is an avid Nascar fan and scrapbooker. Amanda currently resides in St. Albert, Alberta.

Melissa Hermes

Melissa Hermes is a Returned Peace Corps Volunteer who served in Chad, Central Africa. She began working as the Museum Education Coordinator for the Otter Tail County Historical Society in 1991, researching, creating and delivering museum programs to thousands of people each year. She has written for the Fergus Falls Daily Journal, Lake and Home magazine, In Good Company magazine, Fergus Falls Magazine and appeared in the Twin Cities Public Television documentary "NorthStar: Minnesota's Black Pioneers," discussing her research on the African American history of Otter Tail County. Melissa recently spoke about Creative Museums at the Rural Arts and Culture Summit held at the University of Minnesota, Morris campus and delivered an address on Scottish influence in Minnesota to the Fargo Moorhead Saint Andrew's Society. She has a degree in French from Colorado State University and a Master of Arts in Curriculum and Instruction from the University of St. Thomas in Saint Paul, Minnesota.

Sacrifice in Second World War Gander: The Death of Sir Frederick Banting and the First Canadians Buried in the Commonwealth War Graves

by

Dr. Lisa M. Daly

Gander, Newfoundland, was once known as the Crossroads of the World. Prior to the jet age, Gander was a refueling hub for all trans-Atlantic flights and thousands of aircraft would pass through the central Newfoundland town every year. With the advent of more fuel-efficient engines, Gander's role in aviation diminished as aircraft could fly non-stop from large cities like New York and Toronto to London and Paris. When Arrow Air 1285 crashed just after takeoff from Gander Airport on 12 December 1985, killing all 256 passengers and crew on board, the future of the airport was uncertain. The airport continued on, with some military aircraft, smaller, luxury aircraft, and small airlines that serviced Atlantic Canada using the airstrips that once saw hundreds of B-24 bombers take off. On 11 September 2001, as airspace over the United States closed, thirty-eight aircraft landed in Gander, bringing 7000 unexpected visitors who needed to be housed and fed by the residents of Gander and surrounding communities. In the wake of the 9/11 tragedy, the story of the stranded passengers in Gander became a reminder of the good in people and showed the world what hospitality means in Newfoundland and Labrador. *The Day the World Came to Town: 9/11 in Gander, Newfoundland,* by Jim DeFede, highlighted that hospitality, and now, the hit Broadway musical *Come from Away* has brought new fame to the town. Fans of the musical have been traveling to Gander to sample the warmth and friendliness of the community, visiting the North Atlantic Aviation Museum, and seeing all of the sights mentioned in the book and musical through 911 Gander Beyond Words Tours. This has all given the town of Gander the opportunity to once again demonstrate why they were once the Crossroads of the World.

Gander, Newfoundland, began with the construction of an airstrip that would grow into a vibrant community during the Second World War. Newfoundland was a dominion of Britain during the war era, and Gander saw Newfoundlanders, Canadians, British, and Americans all living and working on the base. Thousands of aircraft and crews passed through Gander, and while the airbase was far from the war theatre, it too saw tragedies. Throughout the war there were plane crashes and incidents that claimed the lives of service personnel and civilians. While the airbase did not see combat, many sacrifices were made as part of the war effort. A plane crashing was the most common cause of death, and if the aircraft crashed over land, every effort was made to recover those on board. The first fatalities came in 1941 with the crash of Royal Air Force (RAF) Ferry Command Hudson T9449 and the Royal Canadian Air Force (RCAF) Digby 742. These two incidents resulted in the deaths of eight servicemen and civilian Sir Frederick Banting. From these two incidents came the realization that fatalities would happen out of the airbase, and thus authorities established a cemetery at Gander, presently the only official Commonwealth War Graves Commission cemetery in North America.

Prior to the Second World War, a surveyor selected a location to build an airstrip in what was to become Gander, Newfoundland (figure 1). The plateau and low fog of the area made it a suitable location for runway construction.[1] It was a project proposed by Canada, Britain, the Irish Free State, and Newfoundland, which was a dominion of Britain with a commission government; not yet a province of Canada. This would shorten mail delivery times from the United Kingdom to North America. Newfoundland is geographically the closest point of North America to Europe, so it had been used by aviators looking to cross the Atlantic since the Great Atlantic Air Race of 1919. An airstrip in Harbour Grace, Newfoundland, was used by such famous aviators as Amelia Earhart, Erroll Boyd, and Eddie Rickenbacker throughout the 1920s and into the 1930s. The selected area for the new airport was at milepost 213 on the railroad line and home to Hattie's Camp, a logging and railroad camp, but was not a community.[2] Over the course of the airport's construction, temporary residences, then rail cars, then more permanent structures sprang up. When the Second World War started, while the basic infrastructure was completed, there was a general assumption at the airport that further construction would cease, but officials saw the potential importance of trans-Atlantic aviation and efforts to complete the airport not only continued but increased. At the height of the war, the Newfoundland Airport (later named the Gander Airport) became a vibrant community of Canadians, Americans, British, and Newfoundlanders who all worked and served at the base. In 1941, Gander was just starting out as a trans-Atlantic airport. The previous November, the first attempt at ferrying aircraft from Gander was a success when seven Hudson bombers safely few from Gander to Aldergrove, Ireland, after which regular ferry service started. The first flights were carried out by the Canadian Pacific Rail Air Service Department which was then taken over by the British Ministry of Aircraft Production. This was the start of the Atlantic Ferry Organization (ATFERO), which over the course of the war became RAF Ferry Command. Ferry Command was responsible for delivering aircraft from the North American production facilities to the war theatre. Canadian-made aircraft could be flown directly to Gander, Newfoundland, but as the United States had not entered the war, American-aircraft could not be flown into countries at war, such Canada or Newfoundland, due to their neutrality laws. Horses pulled Hudson bombers over the border from the United States to Manitoba, then delivered to Dorval, Quebec, where pilots then flew them to Gander. At Gander, they were refueled and flown overseas. This helped eliminate the risk and time associated with building the aircraft in North America, disassembling them for crating and transshipment overseas through the U-boat infested waters of the Atlantic, reassembling the aircraft if the ship made it overseas, and testing the aircraft prior to allowing it in combat. The risks to this method were so great that even if only three of the seven Hudsons had survived that first flight, the attempt would have been called a success, and ferrying would have begun.[3] The early flights were, for the most part, successful, but as flights became more numerous, accidents happened. The first incident was minor, but in February 1941, the first fatalities out of Gander occurred. Months later, another accident claimed the lives of aviators. The founding of the cemetery in Gander was one of the first steps in shifting Gander from being just an airbase to a community.

The first major incident in Gander attracted international attention as it resulted in the death of Sir Frederick Banting, the co-discoverer of insulin, who was doing work and research for the war effort. Banting felt that his skills were of best use in the UK, whereas the Canadian government and Banting's colleagues wanted him to remain in Canada to ensure his safety. Rather than abiding by those wishes, Banting used his influence to secure passage to the UK. At a cocktail party, he spoke with Air Vice-Marshal A. A. L. Cuffe, who suggested he fly across with the relatively newly formed ferry service Banting was to be only the third passenger to be ferried by air.[4]

Banting joined Captain Joseph C. Mackey, a civilian employed with the United States Army Air Corps from Kansas City, USA, radio officer William Snailham of Bedford, Nova Scotia, and Pilot Officer William Bird of Kidderminster, England as co-pilot. The crew flew on Hudson T9449 from St. Hubert, Quebec, to Gander, Newfoundland. Trapped in Gander due to poor weather, the crew and Banting had an opportunity to get to know one another, and, rather than seeing Banting as a liability, the crew began to form a level of camaraderie and respect.[5]

On 20 February, 1941, the weather cleared, and the pilots received normal flight forecasts by Patrick D. McTaggart-Cowan, the base meteorologist, in preparation for that night's flight. At the time of the takeoff, there was a light overcast that still allowed for stars to be seen, and a very light snowfall. Overall, the flight conditions *en route* to England were believed to be favourable.[6] The aircraft were inspected both before the flight and the day previous. Engineer Jerome Coulombe inspected the aircraft, but also talked to Mackey about it. Mackey told him "the engine was working good and not to touch it," that the aircraft idled a bit fast, and that one of his tachometers was a bit sticky. Mackey also said that "he flew it this far and he was going to fly it the rest of the way over as it was."[7] The day before the flight, Mackey did ask that the plug for the driftsight be fixed, which did happen. There was no certificate of air worthiness issued, but Coulombe gave Mackey a verbal report.

That evening, T. M. McGrath, the Airport Operations Officer, watched the aircraft takeoff, with Banting's Hudson being the last of the five to leave at 0030 GMT.[8] He noted that the aircraft had a "wavery take-off & did left turn very low but went up out of sight—used all runway & pulled up sharply."[9] At 0053 GMT, McGrath obtained a short wave bearing of 59°, which indicated the aircraft was very close to the proper route. According to Mackey's witness statement, about twenty-five minutes into the flight, the left engine failed when they were around twenty-five miles over the ocean. Mackey turned back toward the airport and then requested a series of magnetic reciprocal bearings, the magnetic headings needed to reach the station, at 0058 GMT. Mackey received the bearings, and about this time, either smoke started pouring out of the control box or an engine exploded and covered the windshield with oil. Mackey gave conflicting reports in his witness statement during the inquiry and to Constable Gilbert Hiscock when Hiscock met him in Musgrave Harbour. Either way, when Mackey's field of view was impaired, he ordered the crew to "throw out baggage and don parachutes."[10]

The aircraft stated to drop, and altitude was at around 5000 feet when the right engine began to give out. When altitude dropped to 2500 feet, Mackey called to Snailham and gave the order for everyone to jump; Snailham confirmed the order. He could not look away from the instruments, so could not confirm if anyone had jumped. The right engine continued to lose power, and Mackey decided it was impossible for him to leave the seat even to put on a parachute, let alone bail out. When the aircraft hit the first tree, he shut off the right engine and attempted to keep the aircraft right throughout the crash.[11] According to a later report,[12] the aircraft came in from a south east direction and struck the snow on Seven Mile Pond (sometimes called Banting Lake) about 100 yards from the woods and hopped a distance of 70 yards when it struck a rock (figure 2). The impact took off the rear wheel. The aircraft kept moving and the port wing collided with trees for 40 yards, knocking them down. The plane swerved, and finally settled, facing east.

In the crash, Mackey hit his head and lost consciousness for what he believed to be about an hour. At this point in the story it is often suggested that Banting bandaged Mackey's head while Mackey was unconscious. This was first published by the *Toronto Evening Telegram* and picked up by the *Ottawa Citizen* and while Mackey himself said it was untrue, the myth persists.[13] Mackey, in the enquiry, says he wrapped his wounded head with his hankerchief.[14] On inspection of the aircraft, Mackey discovered that no one had bailed out, and while they were wearing their parachutes, both Snailham and Bird were dead. Snailham was still strapped in his seat in in the radio compartment with his foot extended through the door into the cabin, whereas Bird and Banting were in the cabin itself. Bird was wearing his parachute,[15] but there is no way to know if he was wearing it throughout the flight or put it on with the order to bail out. There is no mention in the reports if Snailham or Banting were wearing their parachutes, so it is unlikely that they were. There is no way to know why the three did not bail out. Mackey felt he gave adequate warning and was surprised that they had not bailed out. Similarly, if the crew were not even all wearing their parachutes, and did not bail out, it is uncertain as to whether they jettisoned the luggage as ordered. The official reports make little mention of luggage found in the aircraft, but Mackey does talk about some of the foodstuffs he ate from their personal supplies and one report notes that a briefcase of unknown owner, a canvas haversack belonging to Banting, and an attaché case belonging to Snailham were recovered from the aircraft.[16] There was also a request put out to look for any jettisoned luggage, but were specifically told to not search for it. There are no reports of anything being found in the record.

Banting had survived the crash, but he was seriously injured. Mackey examined Banting and found that he had a broken arm and a head wound. Mackey cut up a parachute to create a sling.[17] Banting was semi-conscious and talking incoherently. He would dictate letters to Mackey, letters that seemed to be of a medical nature, and had no recollection of being in a crash. To keep Banting calm, Mackey made as if he were dictating. Throughout the next few hours, Mackey did what he could to keep Banting safe, but his injuries were extensive, and

Banting kept trying to remove his flight suit and boots as he wanted to go to bed. The weather conditions were cold, and Mackey feared that Banting would freeze. Throughout the night, Mackey had to prevent Banting from leaving the aircraft on multiple occasions. The following day, around noon, Banting finally slept. Mackey believed that his condition was serious, and if Banting did not receive medical help, he would die. He left a sleeping Banting and attempted to find help.[18] After about two miles through the snow, Mackey decided to return to the plane. He himself was seriously injured, with several cuts to his head and lacerations on his legs. Years later, Mackey described his injuries as "my leg was badly swollen, my back wrenched and my head and face caked with blood" and that it took him nearly an hour to "work on my feet that second morning".[19] He returned to the plane to find Banting missing, but was too physically weak to start a search. He rested an hour, then with difficulty, went looking for Banting. He found him about twenty-five feet from the aircraft, reclining in the brush with one shoe off.[20]

Sir Frederick Banting was dead.

Mackey used Banting's coat to cover the body and left him there to be recovered by a search crew.

Meanwhile, the search for the aircraft had commenced, but ran into trouble with the poor weather conditions.[21] At 0900 on 21 February, the RCAF made a test flight to see if the weather conditions were suitable for a search. This aircraft returned within fifteen minutes due to poor visibility and the search was delayed until three Digby aircraft could take off at 1400. These aircraft searched the area around Gander Bay as there were some reports that an aircraft was heard overhead around the time Banting's aircraft lost contact.[22] After three hours, the aircraft returned without finding the crash. Over the next two days, the search widened, and aircraft began searching further west.[23] When the crash was ultimately located four days after the crash, it was in line with the bearings given as the aircraft turned back toward the airport.[24]

Mackey, who had survived these four days alone at the crash site with the bodies of his crew and Sir Frederick, stated that he was dazed throughout the whole ordeal, most likely from his injuries and the cold. He could find nothing suitable to light a fire because all the wood in the area was wet due to the snow, but he did have two gallons of gasoline ready to throw on the ground and light if he thought it would be seen by a passing aircraft. Airplanes were searching for the wreckage, but the aircraft had landed next to a pond, tight to a grove of trees, reducing visibility from the sky. The falling snow obscured the crash site from searching aircraft. On the fourth day after the accident, Mackey decided he would leave for good. He tied extra clothing, the aircraft's compass, and his pack to a piece of metal cowling and began to drag it behind him.[25] He was only about 300 yards from the crash site when he heard an aircraft. He ran back and lit the gasoline. The fire blazed, but Mackey was certain that the would-be rescuers had not seen it.[26] Captain James W.M. Allison was flying a Hudson bomber when he saw a wisp of smoke around 1010 and located the crash. Allison notified Gander and circled until other aircraft arrived and dropped provisions and a sleeping pack. While the aircraft were circling, Mackey stamped out a note in the snow that read "3 dead - Joe," naming himself as the sole survivor. A note dropped with the provisions told him that trappers were on the way to him. The trappers, Dalton Abbott, Walter Hicks, Harold Hicks, and Tobias Mouland, found him and tied him to a sled to bring him to Musgrave Harbour. When met by more trappers, Victor Guy, Oudison Mouland, and Donald Guy, Mackey requested that the second group of trappers go to the site and remove the bodies. At about 0200, the bodies arrived at Musgrave Harbour, the nearest community. Mackey arrived at about 2200 and was put in the care of the district nurse, Nurse Parsons. Parsons assessed that Mackey had severe injuries and needed to get to the hospital in Gander, but poor weather kept him at Musgrave Harbour until 28 February, eight days after the initial crash.[27]

Reaching the site was difficult for rescuers, even after knowing its location. All of the available aircraft at Gander had wheels, and the crash was in an area covered in snow, which was unsuitable for such craft (figure 3). Douglas Fraser, the first to land at Gander Airport when it was first being built, worked for the Newfoundland Government and had a Fox Moth on skis. Fraser received the request, and on 24 February, picked up Captain D. C. T. Bennett from Gander and brought him to the scene around 1630 the same day. Bennett had two main tasks in mind. First, he had to get Mackey to Gander for medical attention. Second, he had to find the diplomatic documents that had been on that intended overseas flight. Trappers had already seen to Mackey and Bennett did not locate any documents. These documents were likely removed by Musgrave Harbour residents Walter Hicks or Victor Guy (both said in the enquiry that they picked up letters) and given to Constable Hiscock, who passed them to the RCAF.[28] In the end, it is believed that the documents were recovered. Some documents were passed on to the RCAF, but Constable Hiscock in Carmanville, Constable Wellon in Wesleyville, Acting Sergeant Richards in Greenspond, and Constable Harvey in Fogo were told to report any possible jettisoned luggage or letters found to the RCAF, but that there was no need to search for said luggage (figure 4).[29]

In Musgrave Harbour, before Mackey and the bodies of Snailham, Bird, and Banting were sent to Gander, a small funeral service was held at the church at Mackey's request. The bodies of Banting and Bird were taken to the Orange Hall. Reverend Mitchinson presided over the service. The bodies were placed on a hearse, and a procession, including a brass band, brought the remains to the aircraft that would bring them to Gander. Snailham's remains were not included in this, possibly because they were not as well-preserved as those of Bird and Banting.[30]

On 25 February, Magistrate Hollett, Head Constable Humber, and Miss Carter, stenographer, arrived in Gander to conduct the Newfoundland portion of the inquest. This focused on the deaths of Banting, Snailham, and Bird, not on the cause of the crash. The bodies had not yet arrived, so the magistrate began by collecting preliminary evidence from airport personnel who were present when the aircraft departed.[31] When the remains arrived, the flying officer for the RCAF Medical Services, Clifford Wilson, determined that Banting received his injuries in the crash, including fractures to his left shoulder, his upper ribs, a probable fracture of his cervical spine, lacerations to his forehead and marked swelling and bruising on his face, but ultimately Banting died of concussion and shock.[32] The evidence determined that

Snailham had suffered a fractured skull and Bird died from a fractured cervical spine, both as a result of the crash.

A military enquiry was conducted and reported by Bennett. This court involved Air Commodore Walsh, RCAF, Stewart Graham, Department of Transportation, Wing Commander Adams, RCAF, and Captain D. C. T. Bennett, observer. The enquiry took place in Gander from 3 to 8 March, Montreal from 12 to 13 March, and Ottawa from 17 to 21 March. Ultimately, the enquiry determined that the cause of the crash:

> [F]orced landing due to engine failure. Underlying cause of the accident (a) failure of the port engine oil cooling (broken tension adjuster ring in thermostatic until) followed by failure of feathering motor on port airscrew and subsequent seizing of the engine (b) inability of the pilot to maintain height on the Starboard engine. In the absence of direct evidence but after obtaining expert opinion in evidence, the Court is of the opinion that the partial failure of the Starboard engine was due to ice accretion in the carbuettor [sic] system.[33]

In lay terms, a lug attached to the thermostatic control spiral of the oil cooler on the port engine had a fracture. This caused the thermostatic control to move to the closed position as the engine vibrated, which caused the oil to pass directly back to the tank without cooling. The oil temperature increased, and failure occurred, and the oil was drawn out through the breather on the port airscrew. Mackey's attempt to feather the engine failed, which may have been due to metal particles in the oil that jammed the feathering pump, or the high oil temperature may have caused the pump to jam. Bennett was not certain that the failure of the starboard engine was due to icing in the carburetor, but without any evidence to the contrary conceded it was a likely cause.[34] Mackey suspected it was carburetor icing, but the enquiry did not find him at fault for the incident.[35] The executors of Banting's estate did bring up the idea that the accident could have been due to sabotage, but the investigation determined that there was absolutely no evidence of sabotage. Roderick Hayden, the representative for Shell Company of Newfoundland, who supplied the gasoline and oil for the aircraft, stated in the enquiry that there was no possibility of anyone getting at the oil to be able to contaminate it, and the person in charge of the refueling truck was a Newfoundlander, Frank Munn, who had been working with the company since 1937. The fuel supplies were locked at all times, and the storage area well-lit and under the watch of two men all night long.[36]

Due to this incident, it became standard for aircraft to carry an axe (it should be noted that T9449 did have an axe[37]), a can opener, and matches stored in a metal container. Crews were advised to start carrying a pocket knife, a flashlight, matches in a waterproof case, and chocolate bars. Mackey faced greater difficulty in the days he had to survive alone before rescue because he had trouble making a fire and had no food available. The lug in question caused all Hudsons in Newfoundland and Canada to be grounded until all could be inspected. A steel spacer was tested and ordered for all Hudson aircraft, and others were ordered to be forwarded to the United Kingdom. The final major change due to this incident was that flying boats were to begin operating at the Gander Lake Base, and one was to be kept on hand for summer emergencies. Finding a float and ski plane was difficult at the time, but the general manager of the Canadian Pacific Railway in Montreal, C. H. Dickens, was working to procure one for similar situations.[38]

After the ordeal, Mackey was transferred to a hospital in Montreal to continue recuperating for a short time. Mackey sold his story to the *Toronto Star*, and donated the money to Snailham's children. Once recovered, Mackey delivered another couple of Hudsons overseas, but retired on 1 September, 1941 from Ferry Command, joined the USAAF, and after the war started his own airline in Florida. The remains of Sir Frederick Banting returned to Toronto for a public funeral. Both Parliament and the press eulogized the scientist. Snailham and Bird were sent to Halifax, where both were buried in more modest funerals.[39] There was no question that the remains would all be sent back to Canada and not left in Newfoundland, still a dominion of Britain and not a Canadian province until 1949. As these were the first fatalities near Gander, there was no infrastructure in place (no sanctified grounds) for proper religious burials. Ferrying aircraft was known to be risky, but the only other Ferry Command fatalities to date were in St. Hubert, Montreal, and were believed to be the result of a training accident.[40] Perhaps it was a level of optimism that made the RAF and RCAF believe that there would not be many fatalities in Gander throughout the course of the war, that those who did die would be sent back to the mainland for burial, or a belief that most fatalities, like those involved in trans-Atlantic attempts throughout the 1920s and 1930s, would be lost over the ocean so there would not be a need for sanctified ground and burial infrastructure in Gander. The other option is that because this crash involved a high-profile passenger, there was no other option but to bring the remains of the victims back to Canada so that Banting could be buried with the pomp and circumstance worthy of his status.

The ferrying of aircraft continued for another few months without any further fatalities from Gander.[41] That said, not all the aircraft using Gander were ferrying flights. Eastern Air Command based a RCAF squadron at Gander to carry out anti-submarine patrols and convoy escort work in the North Atlantic. These flights would involve aircraft leaving Gander and flying near the convoys departing from St. John's and other ports, watching for U-boats, and engaging when necessary. The aircraft would patrol as far out into the ocean as fuel would allow before turning back to base. As the war progressed, the distance these patrols could cover grew until a handover to UK-based patrols could happen mid-ocean, ensuring better protection for the convoys. That said, the aircraft were not always close to the convoys, as sometimes the convoys were better served by the aircraft hunting U-boats or attempting to chase them away from the naval and supply ships.[42]

Tragedy again stuck on 26 July 1941 with the crash of RCAF Douglas Digby 742 that resulted in the deaths of six Canadian airmen. The high-energy crash happened as the aircraft was approaching the runway in deteriorating weather and crashed in a bog very near the airport (figure 5). These airmen were the first to be buried in Gander and the remains of their aircraft still rests on the bog.

Digbys 742 and 756 were on anti-submarine patrol, Digby 742 having taken off at 1626, and were called back due to deteriorating weather. At 1955, Wing Commander F. P. Holliday noted a heavy overcast and made a weather check. The Meteorological Office predicted that the storm was localized and that the ceiling would not fall any lower than 2500 feet. At 2050, the weather began to turn poorly. McTaggart-Cowan of the Meteorological Office reported lowering cloud, but no precipitation. The Meteorological Office contacted the aircraft as they predicted the ceiling would remain at about 1500 feet with showers. At 2056, the aircraft were recalled, but Digby 742 did not immediately respond to Gander Station. The recall was repeated twice by Gander Station and again twice by RCAF Station, Sydney. It was not until 2200 that Digby 742 responded, and at 2321, the aircraft was within range of Gander. The ceiling had deteriorated to 200 feet with rain and increased wind, and while Airport Control could see Digby 742, the aircraft reported that it could not see the runway. Cloud had begun to blow across and obscure the runway.[43]

When Digby 742 arrived, Digby 756 was already attempting to land, so Digby 742 was instructed to circle until Digby 756 had landed. Digby 756 landed safely at 2349, but Digby 742 was out of communication range and it took twenty minutes to contact the circling aircraft. As weather conditions were continuing to deteriorate, Captain Tomsett was instructed to head to their alternate airport at Dartmouth, Nova Scotia, where conditions were much more favourable. Tomsett stated he would attempt Gander one final time and if that was unsuccessful, he would proceed to Dartmouth. At 0040, a loud explosion sounded, and command received no further communication with the aircraft. At 0100, the weather started to clear, and the ceiling began to steadily rise, becoming 1400 feet by 0300.[44]

Unlike the Hudson that had carried Banting, Digby 742 was not difficult to locate. At first light, two aircraft took to the skies and spotted the wreck almost immediately after takeoff. Also, unlike Hudson T9449, Digby 742 crashed in the summer in a large bog, so the aircraft was not hidden by trees or snow *figure 6 and 7). As soon as the aircraft was located, a ground party, which had been organized during the night, left for the accident. The Medical Officer for the RCAF Station Hospital, Flight Lieutenant MacLennan, was part of this operation and was present to assess the injuries of the crew. Unfortunately, the ground party found that all six crew were dead on the scene (Table). The remains were scattered throughout the site, and some were thrown as far as 240 feet from the main wreckage, giving testament to the violence of the crash. Fragments of the aircraft were located by archaeologists in 2010 about the same distance from the main area of wreckage, suggesting that this was the location where some remains were found. These aircraft fragments were submerged in an open part of the bog (open water), so they could not be identified. At least one fragments looked like engine cowling.[45]

Crew of RCAF Digby 724					
Name	**Rank**	**Serial No.**	**Duty**	**Date of Birth**	**Hometown**
Martin Edward Tomsett	Flight Lieutenant	C1069	First Pilot	05 Jul 1914	Regina, Saskatchewan
William Hume Mather	Pilot Officer	J3479	Second Pilot	14 Nov 1915	Tunbridge Wells, Kent, England
Allan Gower Pratt	Pilot Officer	J6031	Navigator	05 Mar 1919	Winnipeg, Manitoba
Mervyn Samuel Hunt	Sergeant	R60720	Air Gunner	05 Dec 1918	Calgary, Alberta
Ronald Laird McDavid	Sergeant	R73032	Air Gunner	05 Oct 1916	Flat Lands, New Brunswick
Thomas James Larmour Crawford	Aircraftman 1st Class	R65841	Wireless Operator	30 May 1908	Toronto, Ontario

MacLennan determined that all crew, except Sergeant MacDavid, had died upon impact; MacDavid survived the crash, but he succumbed to his injuries before help arrived. It is not recorded how long MacDavid lived after the crash. All crew were in a state of *rigor mortis* when examined by MacLennan, but the Medical Officer determined that all crew, except Aircraftman 1st Class Crawford, had fractures to the skull and long bones that had caused their deaths. Crawford suffered massive trauma to the abdominal and thoracic areas, which was listed as his cause of death.[46]

The investigation into the crash indicated that the engines were in good condition and that the aircraft had passed inspection prior to the flight. The altimeter settings had been passed on to the aircraft more than once, but Digby 742 never acknowledged receiving the information. The inquiry report lists the cause of the accident:

> From the furrow cut in the ground it appears that the starboard wing tip struck the ground after which the aircraft cartwheeled resulting in wing, nose and engines being torn from the fuselage and the fuselage breaking in the centre behind the bomb-bay.
>
> Pilot attempted to effect landing under bad weather conditions. While making a turn at night at low altitude the aircraft lost further altitude and the right wing-tip struck the ground resulting in crash.[47]

Interestingly, this site has remained relatively untouched since the incident. As bogs are very slow to change, the furrows created by the initial crash in 1941 are still visible on the landscape. The aircraft itself sits on the bog in much the same as it did after the crash. The heavier pieces sank before accident investigation photographs were taken, and the pieces that "float" on the bog are virtually unchanged since the event.[48]

The aircraft crashed only two miles east of the airbase, so the RCAF requested salvaging of the aircraft. Given that the aircraft was in a large, floating bog, Eastern Air Command in Halifax determined that the salvage value of the engines would not justify the expenditure necessary to drain the bog. On a similar thought, the six-hundred-pound bombs the aircraft carried sank into the bog, and the report states that the bombs would soon rust through and could be left in the bog. The bombs should become inert, and in the meantime, personnel were to avoid the area.[49] Graffiti on the site indicates that there have been visitors to the area, particularly between 1961 and 1968 and again between 1983 and 1999. These time frames coincide with the construction and active operation of the Circularly Disposed Antenna Array[50], which was opened in 1970, and the active use of an antenna near the site which was inactive in the 1980s and active again in 2000.[51] Bogs tend to be abiotic environments, so there is some concern that these bombs may not have rusted through. Until they have been determined to have rusted through, the site should be approached with caution.[52]

Recommendations typically came out of each incident, especially early on in the Newfoundland Airport's history. With Hudson T9449, the recommendations were geared toward necessary survival equipment, but in this incident, they were more focused on minimum flying weather conditions, visibility, and additional training. In this case, there was a list of recommendations to avoid a similar incident:

> Minimum flying weather conditions of ceiling and visibility of 600 feet and three miles by day and 1000 feet and 5 miles by night be laid down for this Airport and adhered to except in case of emergency.
>
> That the Aerodrome Control Officers should be given some special training to enable them to efficiently handle difficult situations such as in the case of Aircraft 742 on the morning of July 26, 1941.[53]

At the time of the incident, there were no regulations as to a minimum ceiling for landing. Given the low ceiling at the time of the incident, including cloud blowing across the runway, the report determined that only an experienced pilot should have attempted the landin g. The report suggest that an inexperienced pilot needed the minimum conditions of 400 feet vertical visibility and two miles horizontal visibility in the day, and 500 feet vertical and three miles horizontal visibility at night. An experienced pilot, someone with at least 300 hours flying on that specific type of aircraft, could land with 300 feet vertical and one mile horizontal in the daytime, and 400 feet vertical and two miles horizontal visibility at night. Tomsett had 475 hours and twenty minutes as a secondary pilot on Digby aircraft, but only seven hours and fifty minutes as the first pilot on Digbys. Including other flying time, Tomsett only had seventy-seven hours total flying time as first pilot, putting him well under the recommended experience for the weather conditions.[54]

The remains of the crew of Digby 742 were recovered, but unlike Banting, Snailham, and Bird, they were not sent to Canada for burial. The Canadian Deputy Minister of National Defense (Air), Sydney L. de Carteret, was present at Gander at the time of this incident, and he and the other powers that be determined that more fatalities were inevitable as more aircraft flew through Gander, especially given the unpredictable weather of Newfoundland.[55] De Carteret and Squadron Leader Harold A. L. Pattison, RAF, decided on an area of land adjacent to the airport to be designated the Gander cemetery and was later designated by the Commonwealth War Graves Commission. Crawford, Hunt, Mather, McDavid, Pratt and Tomsett were the first to be interred at Gander.[56] This cemetery was the final resting place of Canadian, American, and British forces (plus two members Royal Australian Air Force members who were on Ferry Command Hudson FK690, which crashed and burned on takeoff on 5 December, 1942[57]) are interred at Gander (figure 8). In 1945, the Canadians stopped using the cemetery in favour of having one cemetery in St. John's instead of multiple cemeteries around Newfoundland, and in 1947, the American servicemen were removed and repatriated to the United States.[58]

If de Carteret had not been in Gander during the crash of RCAF Douglas Digby 742, it may have been much longer before the designation of a Commonwealth War Graves site established in Gander. It can be assumed that as the number of casualties increased, a cemetery eventually would have had to be established at the air base. Ultimately around 150 servicemen were interred (though some fifty-five Americans were returned home).[59]

There were no terms of agreement between Newfoundland and the Canadian Government when the cemetery was first created, but in

1944, Pattison suggested Newfoundland should be responsible for the care and maintenance of the cemetery. Canada had already spent a fair bit of money in developing and maintaining the area, but yet in 1945 opted to use the cemetery in St. John's.[60] Pattison did recommend against moving any previously interred remains, and the Canadian ones (as well as British and Australian) continue to remain in the cemetery.[61]

Interestingly, even though there was the Commonwealth War Graves site in Gander, civilians killed in a 1946 incident were not interred there. On 25 August 1946, a group of RAF Lancasters was returning to England after a goodwill tour of the United States. As the last aircraft was preparing to leave, one of the earlier departures returned due to minor troubles. Civilians would often cross the runway between the Canadian and American side, and those crossing did not hear the aircraft return and failed to see the red lights that indicated they should not cross.[62] The four victims who were struck by the aircraft were Cyril W. Brazil of St. John's, Allan R. Parsons of St. John's, Phillip S. Rideout of St. John's, and Isola[63] Clarke of Carbonear.[64] Perhaps because not all those living at Gander were native to the area (building at Gander started just before the war), the civilians were returned to their hometowns instead of being buried in Gander. According to transcriptions of the headstones, the first civilian to be buried in the cemetery was the infant daughter of David and Marion Heath, who was born on 16 January 1947 and died two days later. Anthony Holland Robertson, who died on 30 May 1947, was the next to be buried in the cemetery. Robertson was from Kirkeudbright, Scotland, so sending his remains overseas was perhaps impractical. It was not until 1949 that non-infant residents began to be interred in the Gander cemetery.[65] By this point, the American servicemen had been removed and repatriated, leaving blank spaces in the cemetery. Those living in post-war Gander may have started to see their place in the community as more of a long-term arrangement or permanent home. Families were being established, and children were being born. As people were putting down roots, they were using the cemetery space instead of sending people back to their hometowns after death. And for the new children of Gander, it was, in fact, now their hometown. This helps mark the transition of Gander as a military airbase to a community of Newfoundlanders, completed by the establishment of the current town a few miles from the airport.

During the Second World War and in the immediate post-war period, Gander, Newfoundland, was known as the Crossroads of the World. A community that did not even exist in the early 1930s became a hub for trans-Atlantic aviation. In the war era, thousands of bombers passed through Gander for refueling, bringing with them soldiers from allied nations. There were tragedies and deaths, accidents, and even a U-boat scare in Gander Lake (it was a boat carrying an oil tank floating low in the water), but there were also dances, picnics, sports, lively debates,[66] and even a few marriages. A community grew around the airport, consisting of a Canadian side, an American side, an RAF side, an army, and a collection of Newfoundlanders who worked on the base. After the war, and with Newfoundland's entry into Canada, the area was taken over by the Department of Transportation and the Newfoundland community continued to grow. During the heyday of aviation, Gander became a hub for commercial aviation, complete with a stylish international lounge that is still part of the current airport terminal. The jet age saw a decline in flights at Gander, but it is still used by various militaries, private aircraft, as well as some commercial aviation. Even with this decline, Gander is still an airport town, and celebrates that history and heritage through its historical societies, museum, and now, through the success of the Broadway musical *Come From Away*. As the aviation industry continues to change with new technologies, Gander will continue to remember its important role in the Second World War, its place in commercial aviation, and its wonderful hospitality on a tragic day when the world came to town on 11 September 2001.

Figure 1: The Newfoundland (later Gander) Airport during construction in 1939. From the Gander Aviation Historical Society Collection, 2018.

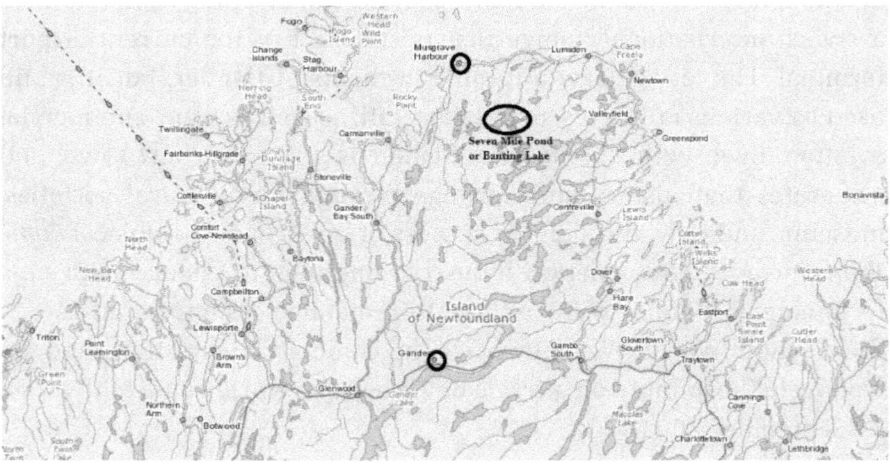

Figure 2: The crash site for Hudson T9449 (Seven Mile Pond or Banting Lake) relative to Musgrave Harbour and Gander (Toporama 2018).

Figure 3: Locals and military security at the crash site of Hudson T9449. This photo is believed to have been taken by Reverend F.W. Mitchinson. From PANL GN 4-5 Box 2 AG 57-2 #5.

Figure 4: Hudson T9449 on the edge of Seven Mile Pond (Banting Lake). This image was taken the summer after the incident. Note how the silver aircraft would have been difficult to spot when the lake and trees were snow covered. (Library Archives Canada 3526812 PA-191367).

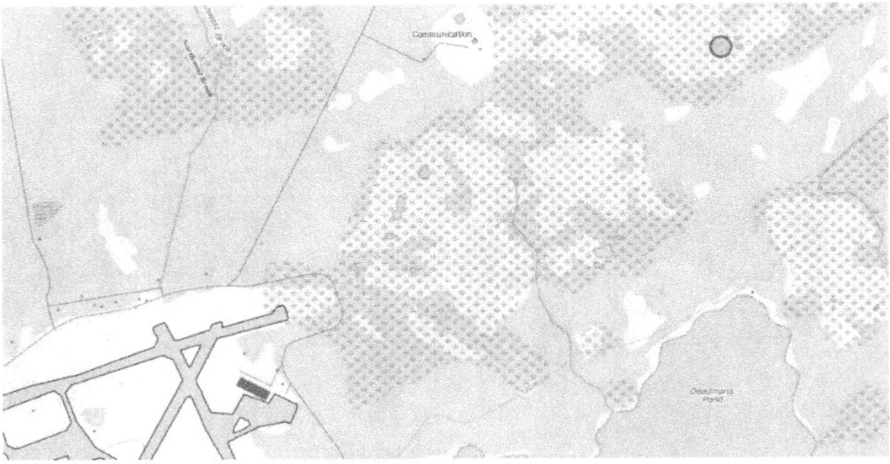

Figure 5: The site location for Digby 742 relative to the Gander Airport (Toporama 2018).

Figure 6: RCAF Digby 742 resting on the bog in Gander, Newfoundland. Photo by Lisa M. Daly 2014.

Figure 7: RCAF Digby 742 just after the crash. Note how little the site has changed since 1941. From Heakes 1941.

Figure 8: The Commonwealth War Graves in Gander, Newfoundland. Photo by Lisa M. Daly 2014.

Endnotes

[1] T.A. Hall and A. Vatcher, "Reports of T.A. Hall and A. Vatcher on Proposed Site for Transatlantic Airport in Newfoundland with Maps". On file GAHS <http://www.gaflight.org/the%20plan/the_plan.htm> accessed 5 April 2018.
[2] Lisa M. Daly, "Aviation Archaeology of World War II Gander: An Examination of Military and Civilian Life at the Newfoundland Airport" (PhD diss., Memorial University of Newfoundland, 2015), 47.
[3] *Ibid.*, 49-50.
[4] Carl A. Christie, *Ocean Bridge: The History of RAF Ferry Command* (Toronto: University of Toronto Press, 1995), 63.
[5] Christie, *Ocean Bridge*, 64.
[6] Provincial Archives of Newfoundland and Labrador (PANL), "Newfoundland Airport 1941 Gander". On file, GN 38 Commission of Government Public Utilities Airport S5-5-1 #5.
[7] *Ibid.*
[8] Christie, *Ocean Bridge*, 65; PANL "Newfoundland Airport 1941 Gander"
[9] Christie, *Ocean Bridge* , 65
[10] PANL "Newfoundland Airport 1941 Gander"
[11] *Ibid.*
[12] Gilbert Hiscock, "Fatal Airplane Crash 10 Miles Due South of Musgrave Hr., February 20th., 1941.". On file, GN 13/1/B Box 398 Airplane Crash at Musgrave Hr., B.B., Provincial Archives of Newfoundland and Labrador.
[13] Darrell Hillier, "Facts, Fiction, and the Death of Sir Frederick Banting:, *NQ* fall 2017, 11:2, 5.
[14] Christie, *Ocean Bridge*, 66; PANL "Newfoundland Airport 1941 Gander"
[15] Hiscock, "Fatal Airplane Crash", 3.
[16] G.V. Walsh, Letter to H.A.L. Pattison 7 March 1941. On file PANL GN 4-5 Box 2 AG572 #5.
[17] PANL "Newfoundland Airport 1941 Gander"
[18] *Ibid.*
[19] Thomas M. McGrath and Joe Mackey, "The Crash of Hudson T9449", *Canadian Aviation Historical Society Journal* Spring 1987, 25:1, 24.
[20] Christie, *Ocean Bridge*, 67; PANL "Newfoundland Airport 1941 Gander"
[21] Christie, *Ocean Bridge*, 67
[22] PANL "Newfoundland Airport 1941 Gander"
[23] Christie, *Ocean Bridge*, 68
[24] PANL "Newfoundland Airport 1941 Gander"
[25] *Ibid.*
[26] Christie, *Ocean Bridge*, 69
[27] PANL "Newfoundland Airport 1941 Gander"
[28] *Ibid.*
[29] PANL, "Airplane Crash at Musgrave Hr., B.B.". On file GN 13/1/B Box 398.
[30] *Ibid.*
[31] T. M. McGrath, Letter to the Secretary for Public Works REF. NFD/106/19, 28 February 1941. On file PANL GN 4-5 Box 2 AG 57/2 #5.

32 PANL "Newfoundland Airport 1941 Gander"
33 *Ibid.*
34 *Ibid.*
35 Christie, *Ocean Bridge*, 71
36 PANL "Newfoundland Airport 1941 Gander"
37 Hiscock, "Fatal Airplane Crash", 3.
38 C.H Dickens, Letter to Air Commodore G.V. Walsh, Royal Canadian Air Force, 25 March 1941. On file PANL GN 4.5 Box 2 AG 57/2 #5.
39 Christie, *Ocean* Bridge, 72
40 *Ibid.*, 309
41 According to Christie, 309, there was another Ferry Command incident in Mull of Kintyre, Scotland, on the same day as RCAF Digby 742, which resulted in three fatalities.
42 Daly, "Aviation Archaeology of World War II Gander: 53.
43 F.V. Heakes, Douglas Digby Aircraft No. 742 Fatal Accident to Above at Newfoundland on 25-7-41. Department of National Defence - Canada RCAF, Gander, Newfoundland.
44 *Ibid.*
45 Daly, "Aviation Archaeology of World War II Gander", 100.
46 Heakes, Douglas Digby Aircraft No. 742
47 *Ibid.*
48 Daly "Aviation Archaeology of World War II Gander", 99-100
49 Heakes, Douglas Digby Aircraft No. 742
50 Locally called the Turkey Farm.
51 Daly "Aviation Archaeology of World War II Gander" 101-102; "9 Wing Gander: History", Royal Canadian Air Force, accessed 28 August 2012.
52 Daly "Aviation Archaeology of World War II Gander", 102; Heakes, Douglas Digby Aircraft No. 742
53 Heakes, Douglas Digby Aircraft No. 742
54 *Ibid.*
55 Darrell Hillier, "Stars, Stripes, and Sacrifice: Remembering America's War Dead at Gander", *American Aviation Historical Society Journal*, Summer (2013): 1; PANL "Memorandum from the Air Representative Concerning the Cemetery at Gander" On file GN 38 Commission of Government Public Utilities Airport, Box S5-5-2 #1
56 Daly "Aviation Archaeology of World War II Gander", 98; PANL "Memorandum from the Air Representative Concerning the Cemetery at Gander"
57 Christie, *Ocean Bridge*, 316
58 Hillier, "Stars, Stripes, and Sacrifice", 3
59 Hillier, "Stars, Stripes, and Sacrifice", 1
60 Hillier, "Stars, Stripes, and Sacrifice", 3; PANL, "Memorandum from the Air Representative Concerning the Cemetery at Gander"
61 PANL, "Memorandum from the Air Representative Concerning the Cemetery at Gander"
62 Frank Tibbo, *The Best of Aviation: 101 Tales of Fliers and Flying as Published in* The Gander Beacon (St. John's: Creative Book Publishing, 1997), 13-14.

[63] Isola's name is spelled three different ways in the record. She is both Isola and Iosla in the incident report (PANL, "RAF Lancaster 35 25 Aug 1946", On file, GN 38 Commission of Government Public Utilities Airport S5-5-1, file AG/57/2), Isola in the newspaper *The Evening Telegram* (No author, "Low-Flying Giant Plane Kills Four Local Workers at Gander", *The Evening Telegram* 26 August 1946), and Isiola on the transcription of her headstone (Newfoundland's Grand Banks, "Bethany UC Cemetery (Part 1) Carbonear Carbonear District", *Newfoundland's Grand Banks Genealogical & Historical Data*. < http://ngb.chebucto.org/Cemetery/cem-bethany-uc-1-car-car.shtml> accessed 14 May 2018.

[64] PANL, "RAF Lancaster 35 25 Aug 1946", On file, GN 38 Commission of Government Public Utilities Airport S5-5-1, file AG/57/2

[65] "Commonwealth War Graves Cemetery Gander Fogo District Newfoundland" last updated 22 March 2013, http://ngb.chebucto.org/Cemetery/cem-gander-com-war-graves-fogo.shtml

[66] Daly "Aviation Archaeology of World War II Gander", 156-60, 209-11.

They Fought for the King: Otter Tail County Men in the CEF

by

Melissa Hermes

"Jimmy"is a former Richville boy, only about eighteen years of age, and a grandson of G. W. Robinson, of this place. He has numerous friends and school mates here who regret the seeming necessity of sending a young enthusiastic, untrained youth—the eldest son of a widowed mother—into the dreadful butchery of the European war. May God bless you, "Jim," and take care of you and bring you safely home to your dear mother.[1]

While notices about boys named Jimmy heading off to service in Europe would have been quite common in Canada in 1915, the above item that first appeared in the Richville, Minnesota newspaper was a new and unnerving prospect for people living in small towns in rural Minnesota. The idea that an all-American boy, born and bred in the American Midwest would end up in the Canadian Army and heading off to fight alarmed local citizens. Minnesota shares a common border with Canada, and Otter Tail County's largest city, Fergus Falls, is only 210 miles from the border crossing at Pembina. This proximity to Canada and the ease with which persons traveled back and forth over the common border made news about local citizens serving in the Canadian Expeditionary Forces a popular newspaper topic.

Newspapers are just one small part of the mission of the Otter Tail County Historical Society (OTCHS) located in Fergus Falls, Minnesota. The museum and research library are considered one of the top small local museums in this state along the US-Canada border. The historical society was formed in 1927 by a group of civic-minded women who built a collection to preserve and disseminate the history of a county formally organized in 1868. In addition to an extensive collection of artefacts, the archives have considerable holdings of maps, ephemera, photographs, and books; church, school, county, township, and organizational records; and an assortment of personal documents. In addition to award-winning permanent exhibits, the museum hosts temporary exhibitions from institutions such as the Minnesota Humanities Center and the Smithsonian.

In preparation for the 2017 centenary of the start of the US involvement in World War 1, OTCHS began to compile research that would culminate in an exhibit and concomitant programming on Otter Tail County in WW1. The research collected would tell the story of small town, rural Minnesota as it experienced the Great War. It became obvious, looking at local newspapers beginning in 1914, that Otter Tail County had a measure of involvement in the conflict long before the United States formally declared war. The story of locally connected men who stepped into the fight early and their experiences as Americans fighting for Canada needed to be shared.

Currently fifteen men with a connection to Otter Tail County are known to have fought in the British army during the First World War. These men had either been born here or had spent some or all their lives in this part of West Central Minnesota. They came from villages like the county seat of Fergus Falls or lived and worked on farms in townships whose names describe the fertile landscape of this eighth largest county in Minnesota's Lakes Region—Star Lake, Rush Lake, Parkers Prairie, and Woodside. While one of the sons of Otter Tail County serving in British forces was an ANZAC who died at Gallipoli, the remainder all enlisted in the Canadian Expeditionary Forces.

The question may arise as to why American men would swear allegiance to the King of England. There were several reasons. Some of these men had gone north to find Canadian homesteads and wanted to fight for their new country. Others had gone to live with family across the border and felt loyalty to the country that had adopted them. War in Europe sounded exciting—some of these men from rural Minnesota wanted a way off the farm and a chance to see large European cities like London and Paris. In several cases, the men were only a generation or two removed their families' immigration to North America. The First World War presented an opportunity to visit their ancestral homelands. For one man, race would play a role in his desire to join the military and serve another country. The call to arms drew in Otter Tail County men seeking adventure, expressing their loyalty to Canada and fighting for freedom abroad as well as racial equality at home.

When the United States federal census was taken in 1910, Minnesota had a population of 2,075,708 with a majority (59%) of the people residing in rural areas. Otter Tail County's population numbered 46,036 persons. The largest population center was the county seat of Fergus Falls with 6,887 people.[2] Both the Great Northern Railroad and the Northern Pacific Railroad lines ran tracks through the community of Fergus Falls. Several Otter Tail County men began their journey to Canada to enlist in Fergus Falls.

Harrison Webster, a resident of Fergus Falls, has the distinction of making history in the fight for racial equality in two different countries, first as a member of the "First 85",in Fergus Falls, a group of African-American Kentuckians, and then as a member of the 2nd Construction Battalion, Canada's first Black military unit. Webster was the son of Allen and Susie Webster. Both of his parents were born in Kentucky during slavery and lived there throughout the Civil War and the Reconstruction period that followed. Although Allen Webster had been far too young to serve as a soldier in the United States Coloured Troops during the Civil War, many of his neighbors from Adair County, Kentucky had enlisted in the Union Army. In 1897, a national meeting of these Union Army veterans, called a Grand Army of the Republic (GAR) encampment, took place in St. Paul, Minnesota. Black Civil War veterans from Kentucky attended the meeting and so did real estate agents from Fergus Falls.

The Kentucky veterans, encouraged by the agents' hard sell of fertile land in Otter Tail County, returned home and prepared to start new lives in Minnesota. In April of 1898 eighty-five persons, now called the "First 85," arrived by railroad in Fergus Falls. Among them were the Websters, including young Harrison Webster. He attended school in Fergus Falls, and in 1910 he was working as a railroad brakeman.[3]

It took nearly two years from the start of the war for the Canadian government to certify a segregated non-combatant unit for Black soldiers. Webster, who was working on the railroad in July 1916, would have heard the news of the Canadian authorization of the No. 2 Construction Battalion. He enlisted in the Canadian Expeditionary Forces in Saskatoon, Saskatchewan on October 20, 1916. On his Canadian enlistment papers, he is listed as being 23 years old and 7 months, 5 foot 2 and 3/4 inches tall. He received Regimental Number 931597. And he was not alone as a non-native Canadian serving in the Black Battalion. One of the witnesses to sign his will was a fellow soldier named Ethelbert Lionel Cross from Trinidad in the British West Indies. After the war, Cross became Toronto's first Black lawyer.

Harrison Webster. Photographed by Benj. Rogers.
Photo courtesy of the Otter Tail County Historical Society [#48464].

The unit sailed from Halifax, and stopped briefly in Liverpool, England before proceeding on to France. As non-combatants, the men of his unit had duties that included, "building roads, railway tracks and bridges, defusing land mines to allow troops to move forward, removing the wounded from the battlefields and digging and building trenches." Some of the men were involved in logging.[4] Webster attained the rank of corporal despite initially getting into a bit of trouble. Within four days of landing in France on 21 May 1917 he forfeited "5 days pay for making away with iron rations" and on 6 June forfeited "20 days pay making an improper reply to an NCO." During his tour of duty, he was treated for a sprained ankle.

Harrison Webster returned to Canada in 1919. Copies of his discharge papers dated 13 June 1919 and a certificate from the City of Port Arthur are in the collection of the Otter Tail County Historical Society and available online at the Wartime Canada website.[5] He returned to Fergus Falls after the war where he married, worked as a janitor and supported his mom, a wife Servilla and two children, Lucille and Ray. He was still a young man when he died in 1930. In an interview, Webster's daughter Lucille McQuitter said that her family believed that his lungs were damaged during the war. Under Circumstances of Casualty, the Canadian War Graves Register states that the cause of Harrison Webster's death was, "Dilatation of the Heart due to chronic Emphysema & Asthma. Died from causes due to Service."[6] The American Red Cross office in Fergus Falls secured a Canadian pension for his family. He is buried at the Oak Grove Cemetery in Fergus Falls with a simple headstone that does not denote his military service for Canada during the Great War. Both of Webster's children served in the US military during World War II.

Harrison Webster with wife Servilla and children Ray and Lucille, photo taken in Fergus Falls.
Photo courtesy of the Otter Tail County Historical Society, [#48465].

Another Fergus Falls resident who traveled to Canada in search of military adventure was Murray Scott Wright. The Wright family was important in the founding of Fergus Falls, with interests in banking and land speculation. Murray had an older brother in the US military and the war in Europe was far more exciting than his dull hometown in rural Minnesota. Murray Wright enlisted with the 212th Overseas Battalion CEF, the famous American Legion formed by the Canadian Army and supported by First Lord of the Admiralty Winston Churchill.

Wright had traveled to Winnipeg to fill out his attestation papers, signing them on 25 April 1916. The Fergus Falls Daily Journal for 10 May 1916 reported on Wright's enlistment:

Mr. Wright joins what is known as the American Legion, an organization composed entirely of Americans, under the command of Major Pittman. He is the son of C. D. Wright of this city, and a brother of Lieut. Geo. B. Wright, of the American Navy. He has taken a deep interest in the war, and has been anxious to enlist for some time.

A photograph taken at the time of his enlistment shows a handsome, dapper 30-year-old man with the distinctive American Legion insignia on his uniform cap. Chris Dickon's book, *Americans at War in Foreign Forces* has several chapters on the experiences of the CEF American Legion during World War I.

Wright's adventure came to an end less than a year after he left home. The Fergus Falls Daily Journal newspaper for 14 February 1917 reported that, "a shell exploding very close to him has resulted in collapse. His jaw is fractured, probably from falling when rendered unconscious due to the terrific concussion due to the explosion, and he has been delirious." He recovered at Moore Barracks Hospital in Shorncliffe, England before returning home. When he died, the

Murray Scott Wright.
Photo courtesy of the Otter Tail County Historical Society.

Fergus Falls Daily Journal for 10 September 1945 expressed remorse at the passing of Wright, "one of this city's fine young." The obituary stated that Murray Wright, "crossed with Canadian troops and was sent into battle while the allied lines were still very thin. A shell fragment struck him, injuring his jaw and causing shell shock from which he suffered during the remainder of his life." For a time, he lived in Fergus Falls with his father, but by 1930 Wright resided at the Bloomingdale Hospital in White Plains, New York and then in 1940, at the Hartford Retreat in Connecticut. Although a state hospital for the mentally ill existed in Fergus Falls at the time, a relative surmised that Wright was sent East for treatment due to the stigma associated with mental illness. The adventure Wright had so eagerly sought had shattered his psyche as well as his jaw.

David Carr of Foxhome, Minnesota was still a teenager when he left in search of his World War I adventure. Youthful and ready to live away from home, he created an international incident when he ran away to join the CEF. The 17-year-old involved not only his mother, but the mayor of Fergus Falls, the Governor of Minnesota and the US Consulate as well.

Born in March of 1898, David and his family moved quite a bit. His father, John Carr, came from a family of early pioneers in Otter Tail County, farming in Woodside Township in 1880.[7] John Carr married Amanda Snyder in 1896 and they had two children Charles David and a sister. The Carrs lived for a time in Wadena County and Hubbard County in Northern Minnesota before settling in Foxhome, a small town just on the edge of Otter Tail and Wilkin counties. Then the Carr's divorced. Whether it was his parent's divorce or the transience of his family, David left his mother in Foxhome and headed to Carman, Canada for what sounded like a grand adventure in Europe,

Once there, Carr reported to a recruiting station and lied to the authorities on his attestation papers about both his birthplace and his birth date citing 6 March 1894 instead 1898. More than happy to help fill the enlistment quota, officers made Carr a member of the 144th Canadian Regiment at Winnipeg on 30 November 1915. David wrote to his mother saying that he was off for the front, and she should come to Winnipeg to see him once more.[8] Instead, Amanda Carr came to Fergus to see if Mayor Frankberg could help her get David out of the CEF. The mayor began by phoning Gov. Hammond in St. Paul before contacting the state department in Washington, D.C. and the Canadian military authorities. Officers in Canada were quite suspicious of the motives of a mayor with such a decidedly German-sounding name! Frankberg just happened to be an attorney and he was able to help Amanda Carr produce an affidavit stating that her son was underage. That document is in Carr's discharge document file for Regimental Number 1084116 at the Canadian National Library and Archives.[9]

Mrs. Carr raced up to Winnipeg by rail to rescue 17-year-old Davy.[10] "My poor boy is in the hands of a relentless Canadian military autocracy... He has told friends he wants to escape from the army they have forced him into. His mother will not desert him in his hour of need!" she dramatically informed a reporter for the Winnipeg Tribune in the 30 December 1915 edition. Hauled before his commanding officer, David was "the picture of youthful western exuberance and health, and any mother would have been proud to see her son in his fine uniform, his eyes shining and his figure erect and strong." David of course wished to stay with his unit to the displeasure of his mother. "Mrs. Carr exercised the privilege of womankind and became very angry to think that she had come all this distance on a fool's errand."[11]

The matter, however, did not end there. The Mayor of Fergus Falls had already become involved in the uproar and contacted Minnesota Governor Winfield Scott Hammond. On 4 January 1916, the Fergus Falls Daily Journal reprinted an article from the Winnipeg Telegram newspaper, "which apparently scents a plot to induce a soldier to leave the Canadian army... The Winnipeg paper gives Mr. Frankberg's name a decidedly German turn, and thinks he was working in the interests of Germany." The mayor emphatically stated that he was neutral. David Carr had again insisted that he was a 21-year-old Canadian who wished to remain in the CEF. "I like the soldier's life, and I am glad I enlisted."[12]

Despite Carr's wished to remain in the CEF, on March 3rd, 1916 the American Consulate in Ottawa sent a letter to the Secretary of the Militia. It read:

> Sir: I am instructed by the Department of State to request the discharge of David Carr, a minor American citizen who has enlisted in the 144th regiment at Winnipeg, Canada. Will you have the kindness to inform me when the release of this young man is ordered.
>
> I am, Sir,
> Your obedient servant,
> John G. Foster
> Consul General

One month later to the day, the Consul General received a letter from Acting Adjutant-General W. E. Hodgins that David Carr had been discharged on 22 March 1915. Instead David Carr, now with a new Regimental Number 829225, had simply changed units, transferring to the 251st Overseas Battalion. He had been, "hurried aboard the troop train with the 61st twelve hours after his transfer and was on his way to the front via St. Johns."[13] Carr would later describe field inspections by Lord Kitchener and the King of Belgium as well as hard fighting in the trenches. He had watched a fellow Minnesotan from Bemidji who lost all four limbs, "carried out of the trenches in a bushel basket."[14] At the Battle of Hill 60, Carr received a bayonet wound to his left leg at the kneecap. "The dead, the dying and wounded were left on the battlefield all night. The next morning dead soldiers and dead horses were piled up together, covered with some kind of fluid and burned to ashes."[15] He described Canadian officers reduced to the ranks while British officers took over, standing behind the troops to make sure everyone did their duty. The Canadian soldiers followed orders because, "[t]o hesitate to kill or be killed or to do anything that might demoralize or stampede the lines means to be instantly shot or cut down."[16]

In addition to his leg injury, Carr had been gassed. "I would rather have been killed outright than to have gone through this," Carr told the Fergus Falls Daily Journal reporter on 19 February 1917. Getting gassed meant that Carr was sent to Blighty, staying for weeks at the Man-of-War hospital in London before boarding a hospital ship back home to Canada. The Belgian king wasn't the only royalty Carr met in person. "Twenty of us were taken out in automobiles and given a big feed by King George and Queen of England." Carr's impression of the Queen doesn't flatter her overmuch. "She had so much paint and powder on her face that I could not tell what she did look like. I hate the looks of paint on the face of any good woman and I know that the Queen of England is a good woman.[17]"

Meanwhile another good woman was again attempting to get David Carr out of the military, and this time Amanda Carr succeeded. Discovering her son's name upon an official list of soldiers returned to a convalescent hospital in Winnipeg, she contacted the Consul General's office. Imagine his shock when Mr. Foster received the following news, "David Carr has been on active service in Europe; been severely wounded and sent back to Canada; that he is now so improved physically that he may be sent to the front again in the near future." Once more the Consul General requested that David Carr be discharged, "on the grounds of American citizenship and minority." This time his adventure was truly finished with his discharge effective 5 January 1917.[18]

While the quest for adventure attracted several Otter Tail County men to joining the CEF, loyalty to Canada and a sense of duty drove others. Countless families worried over multiple children serving in the military during the Great War and two Otter Tail County families had brothers that enlisted in the Canadian army, the Comstocks and the Vogels. Frederick Bertrand "Bert" and John Edward "Jack" Vogel were the sons of Philip F. and Margaret Mary (Hudson) Vogel. A younger half-brother, Charles Joseph Vogel, enlisted in the United States Army Signal Corps serving from 5 September 1918 until 26 June 1919.[19] He remained in the Red River Valley at the end of the war, practicing law. Today, the Vogel Law Firm based in Fargo has offices throughout North Dakota and Minnesota.

The Vogel family roots go back to Germany then Pennsylvania where their grandparents moved. During the American Civil War their grandfather, Frederick Vogel, enlisted in the 192nd Pennsylvania Infantry. In 1878, Frederick decided to move his family to Minnesota to "enter a soldier's claim," choosing a 160-acre homestead in Star Lake Township. The eldest sons, Philip and Martin, helped him clear the "heavily timbered tract of land."[20]

In 1885, Philip married Miss Margaret Mary Hudson, the daughter of Irish Catholic immigrants. Her parents had farmed in Ontario, Canada with their eleven children before moving to the United States.[21] The family appears in the 1885 Minnesota State Census, living near Fergus Falls in Buse township.[22] Within six years of her marriage to Philip, Margaret Mary had already given birth to four children, sons Bert, Jack, and Henry and a daughter. The little girl, born just hours before her mother's death, was named Margaret Mary, too.

In 1894, Philip now a widower, remarried. He and his new bride expanded their family, the four older children were shuttled back and forth between Hudson relatives living in Otter Tail County or Western Canada[23] and Otter Tail County living with their father and stepmother. The 1895 Minnesota state census shows the extended Hudson family with the four Vogel children living in Orwell Township south of Fergus Falls.[24] In 1901, Jack, Henry, and their little sister all lived with their Grandmother Julia Hudson and four Hudson aunts and uncles in Comox.[25] According to the 1911 Canadian census, Henry was living with his older brother, Bert, who farmed at Comox, British Columbia. That same census states that Jack had immigrated to Canada in 1898.[26]

Photograph of Bert Vogel taken before his enlistment.
Photo from *Otter Tail County In the World War* (Fergus Falls, 1919), p.26.

Then in December 1915, Bert and Jack enlisted together and served in Company D of the 102nd Battalion CEF. The unit sailed for England in June of 1916. Jack's Regimental Number is 703896. According to the book *Otter Tail County In the World War*, Bert was a sniper while Jack served in a machine gun unit. While training over in England, Jack Vogel married Miss Mary Eveline Woolley. Together they would have three children. One son, John Phillip Vogel, enlisted during World War II and was killed in action in Italy in 1945.

Older brother Sergeant Frederick "Bert" Vogel, Regimental Number: 703035, passed his medical exams on 26 November 1915 and signed his attestation document on 8 December 1915. Like his brother, he went into the 102nd Battalion. Jack Vogel, "reached the firing line on July 13, 1916... On April 5, 1917, he was wounded at Vimy Ridge, but would not leave the lines and four days later was killed in action."[27] He is buried in the Givenchy Road Canadian cemetery, Neuville-Saint Vaast in France, Pas-de-Calais.

Also buried overseas in a Western Front cemetery is William "Henry" Comstock whose letters home fascinated his friends in Fergus Falls. At the time that he enlisted Henry Comstock had been working in the newspaper trade since 1903 when he was just 16 years old. Born in Fergus Falls in 1893, he immigrated to Qu'Appelle, Saskatchewan with his widowed mother and four brothers in 1905.[28] Before the war he had learned the newspaper trade, working for publications in North Dakota and Canada. From the Estevan Progress newspaper, he moved on to the Midale Vidette followed by the Radville News and the Aneroid Magnet.

Comstock had already demonstrated his loyalty to Canada before the war started, serving in the 27th Canadian Light Horse for one year, a fact that he included on his attestation papers. The day after his 21st birthday, 21 November 1914, he enlisted in the 1st Canadian Mounted Rifles reporting at Yorkton. "After enlisting he helped to get Mounted Pipe band started in his regiment." "In June about a week before leaving for England, he was joined by his younger brother O. J. who wanted to be with him."[29] The initials "O. J." stand for Orrin Julius, and his youthful enthusiasm to serve in the military when just 18 years old caused his mother a good deal of worry.

Now remarried and known as Mrs. Horseman, the Comstock's mother sent her boys' birth certificates to the British government and asked that they be discharged. Despite the fact that Orrin had already served two years with a Border Horse unit, she requested a discharge on the grounds that her sons were not Canadian but American.[30] Her plan worked, but not before Orrin experienced the horror of being gassed in May 1916. In August 1916, Orrin was discharged, "as a minor American Citizen." He would later re-enlist and finished his service in April 1919.

Before their mother's plan could go into effect, the Comstock brothers embarked for France on 22 September 1915, stopping first in England. Always Henry kept in touch with his cousin Sarah Comstock in Fergus Falls. One of his letters to her appeared in the Fergus Falls Daily Journal newspaper. Written just weeks before his death, Henry wrote on 16 April 1916 about playing baseball and football, watching airplane battles, and attending Easter church services:

> I suppose the papers will have published the news before now of the Canadians taking up a new position. We have and from what we are told, it is possibly the warmest position of the line, that is the British line. It is very interesting to us boys though who only came out last fall, since it is where most of the hardest fighting has been done.... In spots one can hardly walk across certain fields without threading his way around—in and out. I have heard that it is wise when the shells start coming to jump in a shell hole, as they never strike twice in the same place, but what is one to do when it is all shell holes.[31]

If Henry Comstock did follow that advice about shell holes, it was unsuccessful. His lengthy CEF Personnel file states that he "was killed in action by shrapnel shell at Hell Fire Corner."[32] He died on 6 May 1916 and is buried at the Menin Road South Military Cemetery at Ypres.[33] His younger brother Orrin was the one who discovered and picked up his lifeless body on the field of battle, a shock that never left him. Orrin Comstock would serve until his unit was demobilized in April 1919. But his experiences during the war remained. In 1922, at just 26 years of age, Comstock used his army pistol to take his own life. The newspaper account of his death and funeral attempted to the explain the suicide in this way, "[t]ogether with the effects of the gas and a term of service of nearly five years it can well be appreciated that he was more or less broken and while he does not sleep in 'Flanders Fields' he fills a soldier's grave."[34]

As deeply as these soldiers felt their devotion to duty and to Canada, in the lighter moments of the war these young men brought with them a love for American's favorite pastime. Despite wearing a Maple Leaf insignia and swearing allegiance to King George, more than one of these Otter Tail County men took his all-American culture with him when he enlisted. Even Henry Comstock mentioned baseball in what was his last letter home to his brothers, dated 1 May 1916, which said, "[p]layed a game of baseball today. We won 9 to 5. Dandy fast game but on a bad diamond. We have a fine little team." Baseball provided soldiers from Canada and the United States with a way to break the monotony of waiting during wartime. James Robinson, born in 1896, had lived near his grandparents, George and Mary Robinson, in Rush Lake township, Minnesota.[35] He moved to Morden, Canada with his mother Rena and brother Walter. In September of 1915 he enlisted at Winnipeg in the 61st Battalion, a unit that, according to the Fergus Falls Daily Journal, "contains the flower of Canadian manhood. The members of the famous hockey and baseball teams of Manitoba, the best athletes of Western Canada."[36] On 24 May 1916 a letter he had sent home signed "Jim" was printed in the Fergus Falls Daily Journal. Despite all the drilling and training and a grueling, 30-mile march carrying 68 pounds of gear, the soldiers still had energy left to play baseball.[37] With pride, he wrote that his unit had "some ball team, and we claim the best that has left Canada. I am the captain and I catch, we beat the Canadian engineers last Sunday, 12-0 before 20,000 people, some crowd, eh. We play the pick of the 4th division this afternoon."[38]

Arthur Elmer Bates, like Henry Comstock, worked as a newspaperman at the time he enlisted in the CEF. He was the editor at the Rural Weekly News in Stony Plain, Alberta, whose motto was, "Tell the Truth and shame the devil." [39] The publication was a "Weekly Newspaper published in the interest of the man on the land, to champion his cause, to teach co-operation among Farmers & to preach the many truths advocated by the members of the U.F.A." The United

Farmers of Alberta (UFA) promoted "Equal Rights for All" in their official song and in the organization, an ideal that doesn't always work in the military, especially a military at war.

Bates had been born in 1881 in Deer Creek, an agricultural community on the eastern edge of Otter Tail County. His parents Harriett R. (Miles) and Daniel D. Bates farmed in various locations in Minnesota before coming to Deer Creek. In August 1910, Bates took a homestead in Alberta under the Dominion Lands Act.[40] He enlisted in the 138th Battalion (later changed to the 49th Overseas Battalion) in January of 1916, receiving Regimental Number 811681. Before leaving for Europe, Bates filed papers to protect his homestead land and named his mother, now living in Fergus Falls, as next of kin before embarking for Europe. His personnel records leave us with a very detailed look at his military service.[41] His unit sailed aboard the SS Olympic leaving from Halifax, Nova Scotia. They arrived in England on 30 August 1916. Within two months the 35-year-old bachelor had married Ada Charlotte Culverwell of Highgate, London, England.

Marital bliss aside, Bates was experiencing health problems. According to his medical records found in his service file, he had injured both his knees before leaving Canada. Joint problems that are easily fixed today with surgery were a different matter in 1916. A report dated 10 November 1916 from the Standing Medical Board at Bramshott Military Hospital diagnosed "[i]nternal derangement both knees.... eight months ago wrenched both knees at tug of war and had been laid up with it for some weeks. Since then has not been able to do heavy duty because of persistent weakness in the joints." The team recommended twenty weeks of duty on base while his knees healed. In fact, a joint injury like this would probably never heal. Despite that, on 6 May 1916, Arthur Bates rejoined his unit in the field.

Evidently his frustrating physical problems persisted and the man who had once written under a banner of "Tell the Truth" did so. His superior officers were not amused. On 14 July 1917 Bates was confined and awaiting trial for two counts of "conduct to the prejudice of good military order." He was tried and convicted of insubordination. Private Bates, "in the Field on the 19th of June 1917, acted and spoke in an insolent manner to his superior officer, Capt. Stack, by failing to salute the said Captain, and saying to him, 'It's no use putting iodine on my knee as this will do no it good' or words to that effect." In addition, when the first charge against him was remanded he replied, "'When a man goes before the MO [Medical Officer], he never gets any satisfaction anyway' or words to that effect." His sentence did not help his injured knees. Bates received Field Punishment No. 1 for fourteen days, a sentence that involved heavy labor duty in addition to spending two hours each day fettered to a post or some other fixed object.[42] Soldiers often called the humiliating punishment "crucifixion."

As his knee problems continued, the Canadian units in his sector were participating in a battle at the Passchendaele front in Flanders. Descriptions from Canadian soldiers who saw action there at the Third Battle of Ypres in October and November of 1917 invariably mention the rain and the mud. On 14 October 1917, Arthur Bates rejoined his unit after an extended stay at the notorious Étaples Army Base Camp. By the time he arrived at the front, the fields of Passchendaele were treacherous muddy bogs. Healthy men with two good legs had problems remaining upright and walking in the mud. A man with two injured knees had no chance. Bates was killed in action on 30 October 1917, although the death was not officially reported until 4 November. His formal will, bequeathing everything, including his homestead and printing operation in Canada, to his wife Ada had been signed on 30 October 1916. She received a pension of $40 per month beginning in April 1918.

His connection to Otter Tail County is tenuous, having only been born here. It is his mother Harriet Bates that brought him to the attention of the Otter Tail County Historical Society. A short newspaper article from the days before health information privacy laws brings into focus the devastating costs of World War I. On 3 January 1918, the Fergus Falls Daily Journal reported on a new patient at the Fergus Falls State Hospital for the Insane. "Mrs. Harriet R. Bates was adjudged insane and committed to the state hospital here Wednesday. Mrs. Bates, as will be remembered, received word some time ago that her son, who enlisted in Canada, and who had been serving with the British armies, had been killed on the western front. She is an elderly lady, and the news, together with advancing age, unsettled her mind. She has recently been leaving home and has endeavored to go to Canada. It was necessary to commit her.[43]" At the end of the war, that same hospital would receive an allotment of 175 soldiers also dealing with mental trauma and shell shock. Harriet Bates never had a chance to talk to those veterans. She died on 4 November 1918, exactly one year after her son's death was officially recorded, and she is buried at the Oak Grove Cemetery in Fergus Falls.

The Fergus Falls State Hospital central tower with portico where Arthur Bates' mother, Harriet Bates, was committed after learning of his death at Passchendaele. She had a mental breakdown attributed to "grief..[44]" Photo courtesy of the Otter Tail County Historical Society [#4275].

News from and about these Otter Tail County-connected men brought the war in Europe closer to this remote part of the United States Midwest. The personal letters and news stories about sons, husbands and neighbors provided pro-war propaganda valuable to the Allies and paved the way for other Minnesota sons to enlist in the United States military when the time came. These soldiers shared so much: the experiences of war, wounds visible and invisible, bonds of brotherhood, love of baseball, or careers in farming and journalism. They even shared similar reasons for serving in the military, whether it was a desire for adventure, devotion to Canada, or the fight for equality that led them to enlist in the CEF during World War I. Just as Americans and Canadians share a common border, they have shared the military service of men born or raised in Otter Tail County.

Endnotes

[1] "Enlists For War: Former Otter Tail County Boy Joins British Army in Canada," Fergus Falls Daily Journal (Fergus Falls, MN). August 25, 1915, p.4)
[2] US Department of Commerce and Labor, Bureau of the Census, *Thirteenth Census of the United States Taken in the Year 1910: Statistics for Minnesota, (Washington, DC, 1913).*
[3] Year: *1910*; Census Place: *Thorpe, Hubbard, Minnesota*; Roll: *T624_706*; Page: *5B*; Enumeration District: *0073*; FHL microfilm: *1374719*
[4] "No. 2 Construction Battalion," last edited June 10, 2016, accessed August 11, 2017, http://www.thecanadianencyclopedia.ca/en/article/no-2-construction-battalion/.
[5] "An African-American in the CEF," accessed August 11, 2017. http://wartimecanada.ca/document/world-war-i/service-documents/african-american-cef
[6] Library and Archives Canada, Ottawa, Ontario, Canada; *War Graves Registry: Circumstances of Death Records*. Record Group 150, 1992-1993/314, Boxes 145-238.
[7] Year: *1880*; Census Place: *Woodside, Otter Tail, Minnesota*; Roll: *629*; Family History Film: *1254629*; Page: *209B*; Enumeration District: *177*; Image: *0020*
[8] "Boy Enlists: Mother Visits This City in Endeavor to Get Son Out of Canadian Army," Fergus Falls Daily Journal (Fergus Falls, MN), Dec. 28, 1915.
[9] Library and Archives Canada; Ottawa, Ontario, Canada; *CEF Personnel Files*; Reference: RG 150, Accession 1992-93/166, Box 1511 - 33.
[10] "Leaves Tonight: Mrs. Amanda Carr Starts for Winnipeg Tonight to Prove That Her Son is Only 17," Fergus Falls Daily Journal (Fergus Falls, MN), Dec. 29, 1915.
[11] "Finds Boy Happy, Lets Him Stay," Winnipeg Tribune, Dec. 30, 1915.
[12] "Blames the Germans," Fergus Falls Daily Journal (Fergus Falls, MN), Jan. 4, 1916.
[13] "David Carr Saw Real Warfare," Fergus Falls Daily Journal (Fergus Falls, MN), Feb. 19, 1917.
[14] Ibid.
[15] Ibid.
[16] Ibid.
[17] Ibid.
[18] Library and Archives Canada; Ottawa, Ontario, Canada; *CEF Personnel Files*; Reference: RG 150, Accession 1992-93/166, Box 1511 - 32.
[19] Victor George Lundeen, *Otter Tail County Minnesota in the World War* (Fergus Falls: Lundeen Publishing Company, 1919), 171.
[20] Meyer, C. M. *FREDERICK VOGEL, Star Lake Township,* page 3. Interview, 27 September 1938. From the Otter Tail County Historical Society, biography files, *F. Vogel-J. Vogel.*
[21] 1871 Canada census, Packenham, North Lanark, Ontario population schedule, p. 40, dwelling 123, family 123, Margaret Mary Hudson; digital image, Ancestry.com, accessed 23 June 2017, http://ancestory.com.

---

[22] Minnesota Historical Society. *Minnesota State Population Census Schedules, 1865-1905*. St. Paul, MN, USA: Minnesota Historical Society, 1977. Microfilm. Reels 1-47 and 107-164.
[23] Library and Archives Canada. *Census of Canada, 1901*. Ottawa, Ontario, Canada: Library and Archives Canada, 2004. http://www.bac-lac.gc.ca/eng/census/1901/Pages/about-census.aspxl. Series RG31-C-1. Statistics Canada Fonds. Microfilm reels: T-6428 to T-6556. Census Place: *Comox, Vancouver, British Columbia*; Page: *11*; Family No: *98 accessed 26 June 2017*
[24] Minnesota Historical Society. *Minnesota State Population Census Schedules, 1865-1905*. St. Paul, MN, USA: Minnesota Historical Society, 1977. Microfilm. Reels 1-47 and 107-164.
[25] Year: *1901*; Census Place: *Comox, Vancouver, British Columbia*; Page: *11*; Family No: *98*
[26] Year: 1911; Census Place: 12, Comox-Atlin, British Columbia; Page: 5; Family No: 45
[27] Victor George Lundeen, *Otter Tail County Minnesota in the World War* (Fergus Falls: Lundeen Publishing Company, 1919), 27.
[28] Year: 1906; Census Place: 12, Qu'Appelle, Saskatchewan; Page: 4; Family No: 27
[29] "The Life Story of Henry Comstock," Fergus Falls Daily Journal (Fergus Falls, MN). June 2, 1916.
[30] Ibid.
[31] "Fields are all Plowed by Shells," Fergus Falls Daily Journal (Fergus Falls, MN). May 19, 1916
[32] Library and Archives Canada; Ottawa, Ontario, Canada; *CEF Personnel Files*; Reference: *RG 150*; Volume: *Box 1903 - 36.*
[33] Ibid.
[34] Fergus Falls Tribune (Fergus Falls, MN), February 2, 1922.
[35] Year: 1910; Census Place: Rush Lake, Otter Tail, Minnesota; Roll: T624_714; Page: 1A; Enumeration District: 0172; FHL microfilm: 1374727.
[36] "Leaves For Front: Former Richville Boy Gives Up Bank Position in Canada to Enlist," Fergus Falls Daily Journal (Fergus Falls, MN), April 6, 1916.
[37] "Richville Man Now In England," Fergus Falls Daily Journal (Fergus Falls, MN), May 24, 1916.
[38] Ibid.
[39] "Rural Weekly News and Rube's Farm Fun, July 24, 1915," accessed August 14, 2017, http://peel.library.ualberta.ca/newspapers/RWN/1915/07/24/1/
[40] Ancestry.com. *Alberta, Canada, Homestead Records, 1870-1930* [database on-line]. Provo, UT, USA: Ancestry.com Operations, Inc., 2016.
[41] Library and Archives Canada; Ottawa, Ontario, Canada; *CEF Personnel Files*; Reference: *RG 150*; Volume: *Box 502 - 57.*
[42] "Discipline and Punishment," accessed August 15, 2017, http://www.warmuseum.ca/firstworldwar/history/life-at-the-front/trench-conditions/discipline-and-punishment/.

[43] "Grieved For Son, Mrs. Bates Committed to Insane Hospital Here, Following Death of Son on Western Front," Fergus Falls Daily Journal (Fergus Falls, MN), January 3, 1918.
[44] Ibid.

Breaching the Gustav Line: The 1st Canadian Armoured Brigade and the 8th Indian Division, May 1944

by

Keith Donaldson

When Canada declared war on Germany on 10 September 1939, the nation's army was woefully unprepared for battle. The military had suffered deep budget cuts in the hard years of the Great Depression, the ground force had been whittled down to a professional core a scant few thousand strong, and equipment was largely obsolete or utterly lacking. In the early months of the war, as the German *Blitzkrieg* steamrolled through Poland and then Western Europe, when the tank proved to be the most dramatic and decisive weapon on the battle, Canadian soldiers were forced to make do largely with archaic machines of the First World War. After a valiant but inauspicious debut on the bloody beach at Dieppe on 19 August 1942, Canadian armour saw its first prolonged engagement of the Second World War in other inhospitable geography: Italy. Between 10 July 1943 and 8 March 1945, the men and machines of the 1st Canadian Armoured Brigade fought their way through the grueling campaign in Italy, from the beaches of Sicily up through the Italian peninsula. Over more than a year and a half of bitter fighting, the brigade, composed of the 11th (Ontario), the 12th (Three Rivers), and the 14th (Calgary) Canadian Armoured Regiments, earned a reputation as being among the best Allied tankers in their assigned infantry support role. In May 1944, the brigade undertook arguably its greatest operation in Italy: the daunting task of overcoming the western portion of the Gustav Line, anchored on the ancient Benedictine abbey of Monte Cassino. Over the course of four days of heavy fighting in support of the infantry of the 8th Indian Division, the Canadian tankers played an integral role in the establishment of a bridgehead over the Gari River that helped open the door to the Liri Valley. In conjunction with the greater Allied assault to capture the monastery and break the Gustav Line, the Indians and Canadians helped pave the way for the ultimate Allied drive to Rome.[1]

Despite the praise regularly lavished upon them by both the infantry they supported and senior Allied commanders, the crews of the 1st Canadian Armoured Brigade have received little attention from historians in the decades following the end of the war. This unfortunate omission has several possible explanations. The first possible explanation is that the Italian Campaign has itself been largely neglected in the study of Canada's experience during Second World War, being seen as merely a "sideshow to the preparation and fighting of the real battle in Northwest Europe."[2] Given this widely asserted belief, it has often been a criticism of Canada's war effort that its army was divided by the deployment of a full corps to Italy, thereby reducing its punch in the slugging match that developed in Normandy and along the Scheldt in 1944.[3] This scholarly dismissiveness has doubly victimized the tankers of the 1st Canadian Armoured Brigade, as they were not only detached from the main body of the Canadian Army deployed in Northwest Europe, but were then also regularly detached from the 1st Canadian Corps to support other Allied troops in the bloody fighting in Italy. Further compounding the issue, only on rare instances was the brigade engaged in an operation as a complete formation, far more often having its armoured regiments instead parceled out to bolster different infantry divisions in the attack.

A second explanation for the paucity of coverage afforded the crews of 'independent armoured brigades[4] in the Second World War is the fact that infantry-support operations smacked of the 'old-fashioned' use of armoured forces in the First World War, and lacked the flair and romance of tanks wheeling in battle in the grand cavalry tradition. Images of German Panzer divisions crashing through Allied defences as they swept through Western Europe were as compelling as they were terrifying, as was the armoured bloodletting that occurred in the pitched campaign that seesawed back and forth across North Africa. What they lacked in glamour, though, the independent armoured brigades made up in versatility. The brigades' primary mission was to fire their infantry onto whatever objective was required, and support them in the consolidation and defense of that position. The Canadians developed a reputation for innovation and initiative that saw them develop new techniques for making their way forward, in some cases in the absence of their attached infantry, to exploit weaknesses in the German defences. The fact that the fighting in Italy was largely an infantryman's, artilleryman's, and engineer's struggle belies the fact that armour, appropriately tasked, could—and did—play a critical role in the Allied advance, and deserves more detailed study, not to mention credit, than it has heretofore received. In Operation Honker, the opening phase to the larger Allied breakthrough to Rome codenamed Operation Diadem, the men and machines of the 1st Canadian Armoured Brigade and the 8th Indian Division proved that close tank-infantry cooperation was essential to battlefield success in Italy, but also that this cooperation did not come instinctively, even for the veteran troops of these two formations.

Operation Honker, set to open in May 1944, was not the first Allied attempt to cross the Gari River and break the Gustav Line south of Monte Cassino. In mid-January 1944, the U.S. II Corps of the American Fifth Army attempted an assault crossing of the Gari, also known as the Rapido, as part of a larger operation timed to coincide with the Allied landings at Anzio. As assault boats and footbridges were destroyed, the attack ground to a halt in the face of staggering American losses. The 36th Division alone suffered over 1,600 casualties, with the dead falling so thickly that one soldier later wrote, "It didn't seem what we were walking on was dirt and rocks. We soon found out it was dead GIs.".[5] Historical criticism of the attack has been both damning and enlightening: "The Americans had failed to seize the high ground, failed to coordinate with the adjacent 46th Division, failed to use tank fire effectively, and failed to neutralize German artillery on the flanks."[6] The fact that this attack failed to win the same ground that was going to be objective of the Indians and Canadians was not lost on the 8th Army planners of Operation Honker. The Indian and Canadian attack, in conjunction with a British division's assault on their flank, was to be part of what became known as the Fourth Battle of Cassino. This battle ultimately saw not only the crossing of the Gari and the subsequent advance up the Liri Valley toward Rome, but also the capture of the formidable German defensive position atop Monte Cassino.

As a direct result of the lessons learned in the failed attack in January, when it came time to prepare for their own assault, the men of the 8th Indian Division and the 1st Canadian Armoured Brigade spent several weeks in April and early May 1944 practicing river crossings and tank-infantry tactics in order to increase the chances of Honker's success. The typical two-day training syllabus began with a lecture for the infantry on tank armament and characteristics, tank capabilities and limitations, the tactical employment of the three-tank troop within the tank squadron, inter-arm communications, and target identification. The infantry personnel then viewed a Sherman tank and received the opportunity to ride it. The following day, an attack involving two infantry companies and the tankers would be practiced, followed by a discussion to debrief the exercise.[7] The syllabus for the Indians and the Canadians also included bridging exercises involving both tankers and infantrymen to ensure that the infantry could be reinforced quickly once they had gained the far bank of the Gari.[8]

There was to be no repeat of the failed American attempt in January, and the Allies prepared as much for the rugged terrain as they did for the German defenders. Though the Indians had already had the opportunity to work with the 1st Canadian Armoured Brigade in the capture of the town of Lanciano in early December 1943, courses in tank-infantry cooperation were an extremely valuable part of the preparations for Operation Honker. The training exercises were important for building morale and camaraderie between the infantry and the tankers, for teaching the new men in the formations the art of tank-infantry tactics, and for providing a refresher course for the veterans on inter-arm communications and movement in combat. The subject of tank-infantry cooperation was deemed so significant that Lieutenant-General S. C. Kirkman, General Officer Commanding the British XIII Corps (of which the 8th Indian Division was a part, and to which the 1st Canadian Armoured Brigade was attached), made a lengthy address to senior officers that laid out the conditions under which tanks would lead or support an assault.[9] For Operation Honker, it was up to the infantry to make the initial assault across the river and to carve out bridgeheads large enough for engineers to throw Bailey bridges over the river.[10] Only once these bridges were in place would the Canadian tanks be able to cross and continue the advance in support of the infantry. As Kirkman's address made clear, however, once the armour had crossed the river, the tankers needed to be flexible enough to push forward without the infantry, in order to prevent the Germans from reorganizing and re-establishing their defensive line. These briefings and exercises were to pay great dividends when the Indians and Canadians finally went into the assault only a few weeks later.

The Ontario and Calgary Regiments began their training with the 17th and 19th Indian Infantry Brigades, respectively, on 25 April 1944. The third Canadian regiment, the Three Rivers Regiment, as well as the third Indian brigade, the 21st, did not participate in this series of tank-infantry exercises. Slated to be in reserve for the opening phases of Operation Honker, they were earmarked for an exploitation role beyond the bridgehead, and had been ordered to hold a static part of the line in the town of Cassino in the lead-up to the operation.[11] Having only been pulled out of the line to rest and refit over the night of 3-4 May, the Three Rivers tankers and their Indian infantry had no opportunity to train together in preparation for the coming offensive. This unfortunate fact was to hinder their advance in the days after the operation began.

While the Three Rivers Regiment was not able to complete any training with their assigned infantry brigade, some of its tankers were given special training in night operations to assist them in their initial role in Operation Honker. This training, which involved practicing night driving and direct firing at night, prepared the regiment to participate in the preparatory artillery barrage that would support the infantry as they established their bridgehead over the Gari.[12] The intention was for crew commanders and gunners to become proficient at picking out lights and the flash of small arms fire through the tank's telescope and periscope and at aiming and firing the 75mm main gun and the tanks' machine guns at night.[13] While the Allies had used armoured regiments as self-propelled artillery successfully since much earlier in the campaign, Operation Honker was the first opportunity for Canadian tanks to provide direct fire support for the assaulting infantry at night, and nobody knew how successful their firing programme would be.

By the morning of 11 May 1944, all was ready. The troops were in their assigned positions, and everyone was anxious to start the show. Operation Honker had been meticulously planned in order to foresee any potential developments in the assault. Detailed planning notes circulated by the 8th Indian Division carefully laid out the phases of the assault, the timing of the various stages, and the objectives. The winding course of the Gari River ran on a roughly North-South axis in the Division's sector of the front, forcing the Allies to develop a plan of attack that had them jumping off from the east bank of the river. In the north, the 17th Brigade, supported by the Ontario Regiment, was to capture the town of San Angelo as well as the adjacent high ground to the southwest known as Point 57 and cut the road leading north to Cassino in the first phase of Operation Honker.[14] In the south, the 19th Brigade, supported by the Calgary Regiment, was to capture two additional points of high ground, Point 58 and Point 63, and dominate the high ground to the east of the village of Panaccioni.[15] Phase II envisioned the deepening of the bridgehead along the entire divisional frontage and the capture of Panaccioni itself. Phase III involved the clearing of a small spit of land named 'the Liri Appendix' sandwiched between the Gari and Liri Rivers on the southern flank of the division's front, and the activation of the 21st Brigade and the Three Rivers Regiment to continue the divisional advance toward the town of Pignataro, roughly three kilometres west of the river.[16]

Reconnaissance reports suggested that the northern half of the divisional frontage was good terrain for tanks to navigate, but that the southern half was not. To ensure that the best routes for the tanks were selected, the armoured regiments received a mind-numbing number of air photos and maps that identified enemy positions, tank obstacles, roads, alternative routes for tanks, and even soil maps detailing the types of soil along the route of advance and how these types would react to rain. It is no wonder that the Three Rivers Regiment war diarist appreciatively noted the scope and depth of the operational planning, but commented that it all amounted to a "bit of a of a headache" for the regimental Intelligence Department.[17] While the terrain west of the Gari was relatively flat to a depth of typically four hundred yards, the terrain became increasingly hilly and rugged beyond that depth as one ridgeline and system of spurs succeeded another. While still theoretically accessible to tanks, the terrain along the 8th Indian Division's front promised to force the Indians and Canadians to follow the few decent roads connecting the scattered Italian villages. The Germans were aware of this as well, and had laid out their defences accordingly. These defences were manned by seasoned and determined troops, including the 1st and 2nd Battalions of the 115th Panzer Grenadier Regiment with the 3rd Battalion in reserve, the 1st and 2nd Battalions of the 576th Grenadier Regiment, and the 1st Parachute Division's Machine Gun Battalion.[18] The Canadian Army's Official History of the Italian Campaign aptly captures the enormity of the task facing the Indians and Canadians:

> The natural barrier of the Gari - forty or more feet wide and six to eight deep, and flowing with the speed of a millrace—[the Germans] had reinforced with an extensive network of wire and minefields along the flats on the east bank. The whole of this forward zone could be swept with machine-gun fire from concrete emplacements and semi-mobile steel pillboxes on the German side of the river. These substantial positions were supplemented by deep shelters to protect the defenders against air and artillery bombardment. Most effective of all from a defensive standpoint was the fact that from the heights to north and south of the Liri Valley observers could direct artillery fire on any force attempted to cross the Gari in daylight.[19]

Even with a detailed idea of the German defences as a result of air and ground reconnaissance, the Indians and Canadians knew that success was not a foregone conclusion. Only time would tell if the Allies were up to the task, and if their preparations had been adequate. At 2300 hours on 11 May, the counter-battery and counter-mortar barrage fired by over a thousand guns from the XIII British Corps and the I Polish Corps commenced, bent on knocking out as many German gun positions as possible before the infantry attack went in. The Three Rivers Regiment fired a total of two hundred and fifty 75mm high-explosive rounds as the 1st Royal Fusiliers and the 1st/12th Frontier Force Regiment of the 17th Brigade and the 3rd/8th Punjab Regiment and the 1st Argyll and Sutherland Highlanders of the 19th began paddled their assault boats across the Gari. The night was dark and foggy, making the fall of shot difficult to observe, but an appreciative note from the officer commanding the 17th Brigade was later received at the Headquarters of the 1st Canadian Armoured Brigade stating that the tankers' fire had contributed mightily to the morale of the assaulting battalions.[20] Still, though, the Canadians could do little more than wait until they received word that the bridges over the Gari were in place that would allow them to play a more direct role in the unfolding operation.

The bridging plan called for three spans to be put across the river along the 8th Division's front: one north of San Angelo in the 1st Royal Fusiliers' bridgehead (codenamed Cardiff), one south of the town in the 1st/12th Frontier Force Regiment's sector (codenamed Oxford), and another further south in the 3rd/8th Punjab Regiment's bridgehead (codenamed Plymouth).[21] Work on Cardiff began shortly after 0130 hours on 12 May, but was so hampered by bad visibility at the bridge site and by the volume of German fire landing in the shallow bridgehead carved out by the Fusiliers that the construction effort was temporarily abandoned. The situation was more promising at Oxford, and at 0735, B and C squadrons of the Ontario Regiment were ordered to move forward from their assembly areas and to prepare for action.[22] By 0847, two troops of tanks from the Ontario Regiment's B Squadron were across the river and in contact with the enemy—the first Allied tanks to cross the Gari, as the corps had not yet completed any other bridgesin its sector.[23] By 0850, the rest of the squadron had joined them.

The Ontario Regiment's B Squadron was tasked with supporting the 1st/12th Frontier Force Regiment in their bid to capture Point 57 southwest of San Angelo, but not surprisingly for the veterans of the Italian campaign, the nature of the terrain west of the Gari greatly favoured the defenders, and made for difficult tank movement. Half of the squadron's Sherman tanks either bogged down in the mud or became victims of anti-tank mines in the marshy and un-swept terrain west of Oxford Bridge. The same fate befell half of C Squadron as well when they attempted to link up with the Royal Fusiliers by way of Oxford, because Cardiff had not yet been completed.[24] The remaining B Squadron tanks received orders to move south toward the Plymouth crossing site in the 19th Brigade's sector, and to then swing west and advance to the lateral road running between Panaccioni and San Angelo. In doing so, they made contact with a group of Indian infantry held up by German machine gun fire from north of Plymouth. The situation on the ground was clearly confusing, as at 0939, the squadron reported that they were engaged north of Plymouth assisting the 1st/12th Frontier Force Regiment, but only twelve minutes later reported that they were now tied to "friends of 14 CAR" (the Calgary Regiment), presumably elements of the 3rd/8th Punjab Regiment fighting their way to Points 58 and 63 west of Plymouth.[25] The morning haze that regularly enshrouded the Liri Valley, as well as the dust and smoke from enemy shellfire and the Allies' own smokescreen severely limited visibility. The fact that all of these units had gone through the tank-infantry cooperation exercises prior to the operation ensured that the tanks and infantry were able to coordinate effectively, whether they were initially assigned to support each other or not. For the infantry especially, a well-placed shell or burst of machine gun fire had the same effect on the German defenders whether it came from an Ontario or a Calgary tank.

Meanwhile, at 0930 hours, C Squadron of the Calgary Regiment was ordered to divert to Oxford Bridge and to then link up with 3rd/8th Punjab Regiment, freeing the Ontario tanks to push north to link up with the infantry battalions of the 17th Brigade, who were having a "hot time" around San Angelo, according to radio messages noted in the armoured brigade's intelligence log.[26] By this point, twelve of B Squadron's fifteen tanks had bogged down or been knocked out, and only three had reached the roadway running across their front. At this point, the Ontario Regiment's Headquarters received new instructions, and ordered the squadron to hold firm on their positions and to provide covering fire for both any infantry in their vicinity and for the recovery efforts that would soon put some of the Ontario tanks back into action.[27] Contact between the squadron and the 1st/12th Frontier Force Regiment remained intermittent at best for several hours, as German machine guns, mortars, and snipers forced the Indians to ground all along the the 8th Division's front. The Ontarios, for their part, were often "too busy ... engaging numerous targets in the area of their first objective" to make sustained contact with the infantry.[28] Despite a lack of consistent visual or radio contact between the tanks and the infantry, the situation improved over the course of the morning as the tanks and infantry, individually or collectively, gradually captured or knocked out the German weapons positions north of the Plymouth crossing, allowing the advance to continue.

A similar situation arose later in the day for the tanks of C Squadron of the Calgary Regiment. After relieving the Ontarios' B Squadron in the 3rd/8th Punjab Regiment's sector of the front, the Calgary tankers reported just after noon that they had knocked out two enemy tanks and one self-propelled gun seen approaching the river to the west of Oxford Bridge, but they had not made contact with the infantry whom they were supposed to be supporting. They reached a position codenamed Highgate, a key crossroads a few hundred yards north of Panaccioni, and hunkered down to observe German movements, destroying several enemy vehicles in the meantime. It was not until an hour later that the squadron finally saw their Indian friends moving up behind them. The infantry had been held up shortly after reaching the west bank of the river by concentrated and determined machine gun and mortar fire, and had been unable to contact the tankers for assistance.[29] Fortunately, while the Calgary tankers were not able to hold their ground indefinitely without infantry support, they had been able to dominate the area for enough time to keep the defenders off balance, allowing the Indians to regroup after their initial assault and to finally marry up with the tanks.

Amid the turmoil surrounding the fighting and recovery efforts west of Oxford Bridge that morning, Plymouth Bridge, the second bridge to be thrown over the Gari, was put in place by 0955. Called a "triumph of mechanical improvisation," Plymouth Bridge was not assembled in the typical manner of a Bailey bridge.[30] Instead of the engineers assembling the bridge at the bridging site, risking casualties from German fire, Plymouth was assembled behind cover several hundred yards back from the river's edge, and then mounted on a turret-less Sherman for transport and deployment at the river. This Sherman bore the weight of the eighty-foot span on an improvised system of twenty-foot steel I-beams fitted with rollers and deployed the bridge by driving into the river with the bridge on its back. A second Sherman then pushed the bridge forward until it reached the far bank.[31] The launching of Plymouth Bridge from the back of a Sherman was the brainchild of Captain H.A. Kingsmill, an officer of the Royal Canadian Electrical and Mechanical Engineers who was attached to the Calgary Regiment. It was the first time that this particular method of bridge-laying was attempted under enemy fire, and no one had been sure if the scheme would work. It did.

Within minutes of Plymouth Bridge opening, No. 1 Troop of the Calgary Regiment's A Squadron under the command of Lieutenant Albert Wells charged into action. Immediately upon reaching the western bank, the tanks came under intense small-arms fire from the German defenders. After clearing a trench system with high explosive shells and his machine guns, Wells ordered his troop forward to the lateral road, where they were supposed to rendezvous with the 1st Argyll and Sutherland Highlanders of the 19th Brigade. Unfortunately, they were forced to advance alone, as a German shell had damaged the bridge behind them before any other tanks could cross, and the Highlanders were nowhere to be found.[32] The rest of the squadron had to divert north to Oxford Bridge and to then make their way south to their assigned objectives, but it would be hours before they arrived. In the meantime, Wells and his troop did their best to locate their infantry, but communications were hampered when the Calgary Sherman carrying the wireless set tuned to the Highlanders' frequency drove over a mine, knocking the wireless out. For their part, any attempts by the Highlanders to catch the attention of the Canadian tankers only succeeded in drawing heavier German fire, and so the infantry dug in on their current positions and regrouped.[33]

At 1740 hours, following a short but heavy artillery concentration in the 17th Brigade's sector, a combined force of D Company of the

1st/5th Royal Gurkha Rifles and tanks from B Squadron of the Ontario Regiment finally launched their attack on San Angelo. The Gurkhas formed the second wave of the brigade's assault and had crossed into the bridgehead captured by the 1st/12th Frontier Force Regiment over the course of the morning, but had been "hopelessly mixed up" with the other battalion due to the heavy German fire.[34] The Germans had fiercely repulsed an initial platoon-strength probe of the town's defences, and the Gurkhas dug in to reorganize and await the order for a full-strength assault. Once that order came, they put in their attack with gusto, but German demolitions hampered the movements of the tanks. A small bridge along the road into San Angelo had been blown, and attempts to sidestep the demolition on the right and left only yielded several bogged Shermans. Despite these setbacks, the Gurkhas succeeded in fighting their way into the outskirts of the town, knocking out seven machine gun posts and taking ten prisoners in the process.[35] At this point, weakened by casualties among the infantry and by bogged tanks, the momentum of the attack was lost. The infantry were ordered to consolidate their positions, and the tankers to dig their tanks out of the muck in preparation for a renewed assault on San Angelo the following day.

The situation in the bridgehead at the end of 12 May was stable, even though the tanks and infantry had not achieved all of their Phase I objectives for the operation. While neither battalion on the flanks, the 1st Royal Fusiliers and the 1st Argyll and Sutherland Highlanders, had reached the line of their first objective, the better part of two infantry brigades and five squadrons of tanks were west of the Gari River. The Ontario Regiment's B and C Squadrons were positioned to cover the western and north-western approaches to San Angelo in the vicinity of the positions held by the 1st/12th Frontier Force Regiment and the 1st/5th Royal Gurkha Rifles.[36] These positions were bolstered by the establishment of a firm base on the lateral road south of the town by two companies from the 6th/13th Royal Frontier Force Rifles from the 19th Brigade and B Squadron of the Calgary Regiment, who had crossed into the bridgehead as part of the second wave during the afternoon.[37] The 3rd/8th Punjab Regiment, supported by A and C Squadrons of the Calgary Regiment, were firmly ensconced on Points

58 and 63, and were carrying out protective patrolling to the south and southwest in support of the 1st Argyll and Sutherland Highlanders, who had become badly disorganized by the day's fighting.[38]

While the opening day of Operation Honker had not gone as smoothly as organizers and troops had hoped, the Indians and Canadians had much to be proud of. Communications between the infantry and the tankers had often broken down or simply not existed, but a secure bridgehead serviced by two tank-bearing bridges had been carved out west of the Gari River in the face of stiff German opposition. The high ground in the centre of the bridgehead around Oxford Bridge was strongly held by a combined infantry-tank force, while aggressive infantry patrolling dominated the terrain south of this feature. When the Ontario and Calgary tanks had finally entered the battle, their presence had made a clear difference in the fighting for the bridgehead. Though San Angelo had not yet fallen, it was effectively cut off by the combined Indian and Canadian assault that had gradually worked its way west and northwest of the town. Further south, marauding Calgary tanks had driven as far as the outskirts of Panaccioni before withdrawing to stronger defensive positions. That Allied tanks had driven so deeply into the Gustav Line positions was cause for much German alarm. Though they had lacked infantry support and had ultimately been forced to pull back, the Calgary tankers had caused a great deal of damage and confusion among the German defenders, and had given the Indian infantry valuable time to reorganize and consolidate their positions.

As happened frequently in Italy, the terrain on both sides of the river had itself been a formidable foe on 12 May. The river had been successfully bridged on the first day of Operation Honker in two of the three planned locations. Mud had nearly prevented the launching of Plymouth Bridge, and the riverbank west of Oxford Bridge was littered with bogged Shermans. At 1930 hours, the Ontario Regiment still had ten tanks bogged down with five Shermans recoverable that evening, while the Calgary Regiment still had two tanks stuck but recoverable.[39] Mines and German fire accounted for five more Ontario and three more Calgary Shermans. It was to the credit of the hardworking members of the regiments and their attached Light Aid Detachments that so many tanks were back in action so quickly.

Despite these difficulties, the Indians and Canadians had succeeded in delivering a serious blow to the Germans in this sector of the Gustav Line. An intelligence report written at the end of 12 May estimated that German casualties from the 2nd Battalion of the 576th Panzer Grenadier Regiment, which had borne the brunt of the assault, may have been as high as thirty to fifty percent of its total fighting strength of 300-400 men.[40] The report posited that reinforcements would have to be brought in to support the battalion if it were not to be overrun. The regiment's 1st Battalion, though, was in much better condition in its positions in the Liri Appendix on the southern flank of the bridgehead. Despite the danger of it being cut off if the Allies were to capture Panaccioni, there was no indication that the Germans were abandoning the Appendix, which explains the forcefulness with which the 3rd/8th Punjab Regiment were patrolling the ground to their south while the Highlanders regrouped. The night of 12-13 May passed relatively quietly, with both sides preparing for the following day's renewed fighting.

The morning of 13 May dawned with renewed assaults on San Angelo and Panaccioni. Both towns presented significant blocking positions against the continued Allied advance into the Liri Valley, and had to be eliminated to allow the drive north to continue. The official Indian history of the campaign rightly notes that San Angelo in particular was the keystone to the German defences in that sector of the Gustav Line, as the demolished buildings and rubble-choked streets made perfect tank obstacles and machine gun nests.[41] Once again, it was the 1st/5th Royal Gurkha Rifles, supported by two troops of the Ontario Shermans from B Squadron, that was to capture the smashed village. Jumping off shortly after noon following a brief but sharp artillery bombardment by seven field regiments, the Gurkhas and Ontarios advanced over the same muddy ground that had claimed five Shermans the day before. On the 13th, the mud continued to be the tanks' greatest foe. Of the tanks, only a lone Sherman, commanded by Corporal Lawrence Toye, initially succeeded in reaching the town. Much of the fighting took place at extremely close quarters as the

Gurkhas cleared the buildings one storey at a time, with Toye providing much-needed supporting fire from the streets. Progress was slow until a second Ontario Sherman navigated through the mud and reached the village. San Angelo was declared clear by 1500 hours.[42] The Gurkhas and their two attached tanks then pushed north to the high ground dominating the 1st Royal Fusiliers' bridgehead, clearing it of a warren of machine gun posts and trenches, and netting thirty-seven prisoners.[43] The elimination of this position paved the way for a renewed advance by the Fusiliers north of San Angelo, strengthening the right flank of the 8th Indian Division's push into the Gustav Line.

In this advance to their initial objective west of the river, the lateral road running north toward Cassino, the Fusiliers were supported by C Squadron of the Ontario Regiment, which had moved through the Gurkhas' bridgehead to link up with their infantry. The squadron and infantry then pushed forward to the line of their second objective, clearing the German defenders from Colle Romano roughly one thousand yards northwest of San Angelo, where they halted to rest and reorganize for the night.[44] Meanwhile, B Squadron moved up on the left of the Fusiliers in support of the 1st/12th Frontier Force Regiment who were advancing on a line due west of San Angelo toward Casa Vittiglio, about one thousand yards distant. In this advance, the Indians encountered stiffening German resistance, but with the assistance of the Ontario Shermans were able to reach a point only four hundred yards short of their objective before the end of the day.

While the 17th Brigade and the Ontario Regiment moved to secure San Angelo, the 19th Brigade and the Ontario Regiment made their combined assault on Panaccioni with the intent to secure the left flank of the 8th Indian Division's bridgehead over the Gari. At 0700 hours, two troops of tanks from the Calgary Regiment's B Squadron were ordered to move up along the brigade's right boundary in support of B Company of the 6th/13th Royal Frontier Force Rifles. Their objective was to capture the ridge of high ground connecting San Angelo to Panaccioni. On their left flank, two troops from C Squadron were to help fire B Company of the Rifles onto the crossroads directly north of the town, in preparation for a direct assault on Panaccioni itself by C

Company of the Rifles and one troop of tanks from B Squadron of the Calgaries.[45]

The advance to the ridge "went through very close country, intersected by leafy lanes and sunken roads, ideal for the concealment of anti-tank guns."[46] In this broken terrain where visibility was reduced, the tank-infantry training that the troops had undergone prior to the start of Operation Honker paid great dividends. The infantry used tracer fire from their Bren guns to identify well-concealed enemy strongpoints that the tanks promptly dealt with. After the Rifles and Calgaries threw back a determined German counterattack that developed around 1300, they declared the position secured at 1600 hours. Unfortunately, while only one Sherman was lost to enemy fire, the attacking Rifles company had been reduced to twenty-five all ranks, forcing the brigade commander to bring up a company from the 3rd/8th Punjab Regiment to reinforce the line in the battered hamlet. With the reduction of the German positions on the ridgeline, the Allied hold on San Angelo to the northeast was secured, and the way lay open for an aggressive assault on Panaccioni to deepen and strengthen the divisional bridgehead.

As they advanced on the high ground and important crossroads northeast of Panaccioni, A Company of the Rifles and C Squadron of the Calgaries encountered determined German resistance, bolstered by several tanks and self-propelled guns. Using the combined infantry-tank tactics of fire and movement honed in the weeks leading up to the operation, and utilizing the hilly terrain to best advantage, the Indians and Canadians accounted for four German tanks and two self-propelled guns in the span of a few hours for the loss of a single Sherman.[47]

With the high ground secured by 1500 hours, the assault on Panaccioni could begin. Despite a short artillery concentration on the town, initial German resistance was fierce. As the attack developed and Allied tanks and infantry entered the town, though, the spirited defence unexpectedly collapsed. Adding to the lengthening list of successes for the Indians and Canadians was the capture of the headquarters of the 2nd Battalion, the 576th Panzer Grenadier Regiment, along with a total of 120 prisoners.[48] With the town secured by 1900 hours, the Calgaries and Rifles dug in and consolidated their defences in an arc extending northeast along the ridgeline from Panaccioni that linked up with the 17th Brigade in and around San Angelo.

By last light on 13 May, the situation in the bridgehead had vastly improved from the previous day. The flanks of the divisional bridgehead in particular had been much strengthened by the capture of San Angelo and Panaccioni, and by the consolidation of a continuous front line west of the Gari that stretched over three thousand yards long. Together, the 17th and 19th Brigades and the Ontario and Calgary Regiments had five infantry battalions and five squadrons of tanks well dug-in in the bridgehead, with preparations being made for elements of the Three Rivers Regiment and the 21st Brigade to move into the bridgehead early on 14 May to continue the advance. The final Ontario squadron, A Squadron, was ready and eager to move into the bridgehead, but was delayed in crossing the river due to heavy traffic; priority had been given to the Three Rivers Regiment and the 21st Brigade, and to elements of the 78th British Division, the XIII Corps's reserve division, which squeezed into the ground won on the 8th Indian Division's right flank between the Indians and the 4th British Division.[49]

A general stiffening of the German defences had been noted on 13 May at the same time as their forces were absorbing larger numbers of casualties—an indication both of the ferocious nature of the fighting that took place that day and of the skill with which the Canadian tankers and Indian infantry worked together to drive into the Gustav line positions. The intelligence staff of the 8th Indian Division observed the piecemeal deployment of much of the 576th Panzer Grenadier Regiment's local reserves throughout 13 May in a vain attempt to stem the Allied assault. This intelligence happily reported that the 2nd Battalion, 576th Grenadier Regiment had been "practically annihilated." In addition to uncounted numbers of enemy killed and wounded, the Germans had suffered approximately 150 prisoners captured since Operation Honker began.[50] On the division's right flank, the 4th British Division had encountered even stiffer resistance, but had captured a further 345 prisoners from a number of German units since the beginning of the assault.[51] Troops had finally managed to throw a bridge over the Gari in the British sector on the morning of 13 May, which took immense pressure off Oxford and Plymouth in the 8th Indian Division's bridgehead.

Integral to the successes of the day was a vast improvement in the degree of tank-infantry cooperation exhibited by the Indians and Canadians. This was likely due to the fact that the tanks and infantry had had time to properly marry up and confer on a basic plan for the day's assault prior to the attacks going in. Unlike on 12 May, when the tankers had to first locate the infantry in the confusion of battle, on the 13th the men of the Ontario and Calgary Regiments were already deployed in forward positions either alongside or very near their infantry battalions, making the formulation of assault plans much easier.

Early on 14 May, at 0100 hours, C Squadron of the Three Rivers Regiment crossed Oxford Bridge and married up with the 3rd/15th Punjab Regiment of the 21st Brigade at Point 63 in 19th Brigade's area, northeast of Panaccioni. The regiment's B Squadron would cross the river at 0400, followed by A Squadron and regimental headquarters at 0500. From this start line, they were ordered to capture the hamlets of Massa Evangelista and Colle D'Alessandro, and cut the Cassino-Pignataro road. According to the Three Rivers Regiment's war diary, the attack was "tough from the word GO."[52] Brush-covered hills and ravines provided perfect cover for the defenders, while mule tracks, deep roadbeds, wadis, boggy ground, and minefields all conspired to slow the Allied troops, and channel them towards prepared German positions. In this decidedly inhospitable terrain, the lack of tank-infantry training between the Three Rivers Regiment and the 21st Brigade became painfully obvious. Determined enemy resistance by isolated pockets of machine-gunners, snipers, and mortars bypassed by the tanks frequently held the infantry up, as they went to ground in the face of heavy small-arms fire. At some points, the tanks wound up as far as five hundred yards ahead of their infantry, forcing them to turn around and retrace their paths through the difficult terrain to re-establish contact with them. At one point, the tankers reported that they had reached a point of high ground three hundred yards north of

Massa Evangelista, but later that they had to abandon the position and withdraw in the absence of any friendly infantry with them.[53] Despite these setbacks, however, the 3rd/15th Punjab Regiment and C Squadron did make progress toward Massa Evangelista before B Squadron and the 5th Royal West Kents took over the advance, and later intelligence reports indicated that the initial assault inflicted heavy casualties on the German defenders.

Unlike the first phase of the attack, the advance by B Squadron and the Royal West Kents made excellent progress, despite continued stiff German resistance. Clearly, the defenders had been so exhausted in the earlier fighting that the attackers were able to smash through the weakening defences to seize their first objective, Point 66, roughly halfway to Massa Evangelista from the start line. By nightfall, the Royal West Kents and the tanks of B Squadron had consolidated five hundred yards further northwest, on the high ground overlooking the village itself.[54] In their advance, the Royal West Kents and tankers knocked out two anti-tank guns, and captured twenty prisoners.

There is little concrete evidence to suggest why this second phase of the attack proceeded so much more smoothly than the first, as little on the subject is mentioned in the Three Rivers Regiment's war diary or either the Canadian or Indian official histories. That being said, a situation report transmitted by the armoured regiment to the 1st Canadian Armoured Brigade's Headquarters reported that progress in the initial assault was hampered by low visibility, due to the morning fog that materialized regularly in the Liri Valley.[55] Combined with the determined German resistance, this made close communication and cooperation difficult between two units unfamiliar with each other. By the time that the Royal West Kents and B Squadron took up the advance; however, the fog would have burnt off, and progress would have been made much easier with clearer visibility and with the enemy already reeling from the earlier attack.

As the Three Rivers Regiment and the 21st Brigade advanced west out of the bridgehead, the Ontario and Calgary Regiments continued to assist the 17th and 19th Brigades in solidifying their hold on their respective sectors. In the south, the Calgaries' A Squadron linked up with the now-rested 1st Argyll and Sutherland Highlanders and proceeded to clear the Liri Appendix on the southern flank of the division's area, in the face of light but determined machine gun fire. In the 17th Brigade's sector, B and C Squadrons of the Ontario Regiment, supporting the 1st/12th Frontier Force Regiment and the 1st Royal Fusiliers, respectively, met much stiffer resistance. This Allied advance drew fire from numerous anti-tank guns, self-propelled artillery, and tanks, with one B Squadron Sherman being knocked out. Retaliatory Allied artillery fire was unable to silence the cunningly hidden weapon responsible, illustrating one of the hallmarks of the Italian campaign as a whole: the terrain worked to the advantage of the defenders, and the Germans were adept at deploying their weapons to maximize both their field of fire and their concealment.

Shortly after the Sherman was hit, a determined German counter-attack developed with approximately two companies of infantry supported by tanks advancing on the Indian and Canadian positions. In the ensuing firefight, each Ontario squadron had a tank knocked out by enemy fire, and the Allied troops were further pushed back on their heels when their supporting artillery barrage fell short and onto their own positions.[56] When the Indian infantry withdrew slightly to regroup, the Ontario tanks, remaining in their positions, radioed range corrections to the artillery. They then surged forward with their infantry to break up the counterattack and sweep the Germans off the high ground before them. By 1700 hours, the Ontario Regiment and the 17th Brigade had secured their secondary objectives for Operation Honker, and had firmly established themselves in the villages of Colle Romano and Casa Vittiglio.[57] In the abortive German counter-attack and the subsequent Allied reply, the Germans lost eight anti-tank guns one self-propelled gun, and one tank for the loss of three of the Ontarios' Shermans. Once again, the Canadian tankers had proven their worth in the close terrain of the Liri Valley. They had provided precise targeting information for the Allied artillery in addition to their own accurate high explosive and armour-piercing shellfire in order to break up one of the fiercest German counter-attacks yet encountered by the 8th Indian Division in the Liri Valley. Refusing to give ground in the face of the enemy, the Ontario tankers had bought time for their

Indian infantry to reorganize and launch their own counter-attack against the German forces on the heights.

On 15 May, the fourth day of Operation Honker, the 21st Brigade continued its advance toward the Cassino-Pignataro road with the Three Rivers Regiment in support. Leading off were the 1st/5th Mahratta Light Infantry, with A Squadron of the Three Rivers Regiment. Advancing from their jumping-off point near Massa Evangelista, the tanks gave "magnificent support throughout" the assault, helping to suppress machine guns and snipers who were harassing and delaying the infantry.[58] Once again, difficult terrain and German anti-tank defences made the going difficult for the tanks, accounting for two Shermans bogged and one tank destroyed, but no crew casualties were suffered. Further progress that day by the 21st Brigade and the Three Rivers tankers left them in possession of Casa Monaco, a small collection of buildings fifteen hundred yards north of Pignataro, and eight hundred yards west of the Cassino-Pignataro road.[59] There they dug in, and there they stayed, until the Indians were relieved near midnight on the night of 16-17 May by battalions from the 3rd Canadian Infantry Brigade. The Three Rivers Regiment then came under the command of the 1st Canadian Infantry Division as it relieved the 8th Indian Division in the line.

To the south of the 21st Brigade's drive, the town of Pignataro fell to the troops of the 6th/13th Royal Frontier Force Rifles of the 19th Brigade late on the night of 15 May. Having decided that a frontal assault on the town in broad daylight would be suicide, even with the support of the Calgary Regiment's B Squadron, the infantry waited until after sundown before putting in their attack. They were fired into the town by a heavy artillery bombardment, as well as by the local fire support provided by the Calgary Shermans. After two hours of shelling, the attack went in at 2045, and the town was declared secure by 2300 hours.[60] Though able to provide adequate supporting fire in the worsening light, any attempt by the Calgaries to engage in street warfare at night would have surely courted disaster. Vulnerable to fire from upper-storey windows and balconies even in daylight, the Shermans were even more defenseless after dark, and so the clearing of the town itself was left to the Indians.

While the fight for Pignataro was sharp but relatively brief, the advance by the Argyll and Sutherland Highlanders and the Calgaries' A Squadron south of the town met heavy opposition in the form of machine guns and anti-tank guns that pinned the infantry down and knocked out two Calgary Shermans. Among the Calgary dead was Lieutenant Albert Wells of No. 1 Troop, who had spearheaded the Calgary charge across Plymouth Bridge on 12 May. His tank was the second to be hit by anti-tank fire as they moved up onto yet another German-held ridgeline west of Panaccioni.[61] As a result of this heavy fire and the decimation of the Calgaries' No. 1 Troop, the infantry and tanks dug in for the night along the line of a ravine meandering south from Pignataro. The following day was devoted to some forward patrolling and the subsequent relief of the unit by elements of the 1st Canadian Infantry Brigade and tanks from the 25th British Tank Brigade.[62] Following the hard fighting west of the Gari, the men of the Calgary Regiment were more than ready for a rest.

The day passed relatively quietly for the Ontario Regiment as the battalions of the 17th Brigade, with the exception of the 1st/12th Frontier Force Regiment, were ordered to hold fast on their current positions and to only carry out offensive patrols in the hills before them. The 1st/12th Frontier Force Regiment, with the support of A Squadron of the Ontario Regiment which had finally found room on the bridges over the Gari, was ordered to advance west to secure the right flank of the 21st Brigade. While they encountered a few anti-tank and machine gun positions, these were quickly dealt with. By the end of the day, the infantry and accompanying tanks were firmly ensconced on Point 82, the high ground overlooking Colle d'Alessandro. Early that evening, the Ontario Regiment was ordered to retire to a rest area established near San Vittore, roughly five miles east of the Gari, for a period of refitting and rest.[63] This marked the end of the regiment's work with the 8th Indian Division in Operation Honker.

At the squadron level, the performance of the individual Canadian armoured regiments in Operation Honker was first-rate. Inevitably, there were instances where tank-infantry cooperation broke down, but the early appearance of even small numbers of tanks west of the

Gari came as an incredible shock to the Germans. In only two instances between 12 and 15 May did the infantry have to cede ground for more than a few hours: following the initial proves towards San Angelo on 12 May by the 1st/5th Royal Gurkha Rifles, and the 1st Argyll and Sutherland Highlanders' withdrawal to the east bank of the Gari in the early hours of 13 May. In both cases, the infantry had been without armoured support. The Ontarios had had so many tank bog down west of Oxford Bridge on 12 May that there had simply been insufficient armour to support both the 1st/12th Frontier Force Regiment and the Gurkhas. As for the Highlanders, they had suffered so many casualties in the initial assault across the Gari that they had been unable to advance far enough beyond the river to meet up with the Calgary Regiment, and had no working radios with which to contact them. Having been given time to reorganize and link up with their supporting tanks, however, both the Gurkhas and Highlanders went on to capture their objectives of San Angelo and the Liri Appendix, respectively.

Aside from these cases, the only real difficulties in tank-infantry cooperation were encountered when the Three Rivers Regiment and the 21st Brigade went into action together on 14 May. The advance by C Squadron and the 3rd/15th Punjab Regiment was greatly hindered by a breakdown in communications between the two arms, with the tanks often roaming far ahead of the pinned-down infantry. Even here, however, while forward progress was slow, the attack caused severe casualties among the German defenders. These losses dislocated the enemy defences, allowing the second phase of the assault to progress more quickly and with more satisfactory gains. Since later attacks by the Three Rivers Regiment and the 21st Brigade were ultimately very successful and showed close cooperation of a high order, too much should not be made of the early breakdowns. Considering the gains made by the infantry and tanks following the initial phase of the advance on 14 May, other reasons for the cooperative difficulties besides a simple lack of preparatory training must exist. First, it was the first advance made by the 3rd/15th Punjab Regiment and Three Rivers tankers after spending several days out of the line. Second, it was made against determined and well-entrenched German defenders.

Finally, the advance was pushed forward in rugged terrain decidedly inhospitable to tanks. The fact that even partially successful attacks could have such beneficial consequences for the Allies in the larger operation must not be ignored. Hard fighting on the 8th Indian Division's front pinned valuable local German reserves to the San Angelo sector and effectively denied them to German forces attempting to stem the Allied assaults in the mountains north and south of the Liri Valley. The threat posed by the Indians and Canadians also prevented reserves from falling back to prepared defensive positions in the Hitler Line, several miles to the rear.

Though the Canadian tankers consistently provided timely and devastating local fire support for their infantry throughout the offensive, it is more difficult to measure the success of the brigade as a whole due to the fact that, as per standard doctrine for independent armoured brigades, the regiments were broken down into their component squadrons during these combat operations. This ensured that all the infantry battalions received proper armoured support, but also meant that at no time did the Germans feel the full weight of the brigade bearing down on them along a single axis. Instead, the Shermans were doled out piecemeal to infantry brigades and battalions as the situation in the bridgehead warranted. Independent armoured formations such as the 1st Canadian Armoured Brigade essentially traced their lineage back to the formations of armoured behemoths of the First World War that slowly clawed their way over muddy battlefields at the pace of a walking infantryman. This support role was not glamourous, but it was effective at the squadron level, Judging from the brigade's intelligence log for May 1944, however, we can conclude that Brigade Headquarters did maintain a firm grasp both of the unfolding battle and of its three armoured regiments throughout the fighting west of the Gari. Within the log, pages upon pages of neatly typed text document the messages and queries that swirled back and forth between the tank troops and infantry battalions, the regiments, the brigades, the division, and the senior echelons of command as the Canadians and Indians methodically went about the business of their assault. With its tanks subordinated to the infantry commanders, the headquarters of the 1st Canadian Armoured

Brigade was essentially relegated to an administrative and logistical role, managing the armoured forces and mustering their attached support arms east of the Gari, and keeping abreast of the progress of the forward squadrons by radio contact with regimental headquarters. The men of the brigade headquarters ably performed this role, coordinating recovery efforts for damaged or bogged tanks, assisting with the replenishment and relief of the regiments and squadrons as needed, and maintaining lines of communication between the tankers in the field and higher Allied formations. Indeed, the brigade war diarist concluded with some satisfaction that on many occasions during the operation, the 8th Indian Division had requested confirmation of reports received from their forward infantry, and Brigade Headquarters had always been able to meet those requests as a result of their excellent wireless communications.[64]

Without a doubt, the efforts of the 1st Canadian Armoured Brigade to support the battalions of the 8th Indian Division in Operation Honker were critical to the ultimate success of the operation. Once the tanks reached the west bank of the Gari, the Canadians quickly set about the destruction of the enemy's defences in the sector, marrying up with their Allied infantry and causing severe German casualties. In the face of determined resistance, inhospitable terrain, and a chaotic battlefield choked with smoke and dust, the overall momentum of the advance never faltered. Together with the infantry of the 8th Indian Division, the members of the Ontario, Calgary, and Three Rivers Regiments played a central role in the puncturing of the Gustav Line as the Allies launched their drive on Rome in the spring of 1944.

Bibliography

Archival Sources

Library and Archives Canada Record Group RG-24
War Diaries and Appendices
1st Canadian Armoured Brigade Headquarters
11th Canadian Armoured Regiment (The Ontario Regiment)
12th Canadian Armoured Regiment (The Three Rivers Regiment)
14th Canadian Armoured Regiment (The Calgary Regiment)

Directorate of History and Heritage
Cardex File, The Ontario Regiment

The Military Museums, Calgary
War Diaries and Appendices
14th Canadian Armoured Regiment (The Calgary Regiment)

Secondary Sources

Atkinson, Rick. *The Day of Battle: The War in Sicily and Italy, 1943-1944*. New York: Henry Holt & Co., 2007.

Cook, Tim. *Clio's Warriors: Canadian Historians and the Writing of the World Wars*. Vancouver: University of British Columbia Press, 2006.

Dancocks, Daniel. *The D-Day Dodgers: The Canadians in Italy, 1943-1945*. Toronto: McClelland & Stewart, 1991.

McAndrew, Bill. *Canadians and the Italian Campaign 1943-1945*. Montreal: Art Global, 1996.

Molony, C.J.C. *The Mediterranean and Middle East Volume VI: Victory in the Mediterranean, Part I: 1st April to 4th June 1944*. London: Her Majesty's Stationery Office, 1986.

Nicholson, G.W.L. *Official History of the Canadian Army in the Second World War Volume II: The Canadians in Italy 1943-1945*. Ottawa: Queen's Printer, 1966.

Pal, Dharm. *Official History of the Indian Armred Forces in the Second World War 1939-1945: The Campaign in Italy 1943-45*. Calcutta: Sree Saraswaty Press, 1960.

Stacey, C.P. *The Canadian Army, 1939-1945: An Official Historical Summary*. Ottawa: King's Printer, 1948.

Zuehlke, Mark. *The Liri Valley: Canada's World War II Breakthrough to Rome*. Toronto: Stoddart, 2001.

Endnotes

---

[1] Fighting as part of the British 8th Army, the Indians and Canadians in Italy served alongside many other nations' soldiers, including British, New Zealander, South African, Polish, Palestinian, Maltese, and even Italian troops. While this fact has been noted by numerous historians, it remains a truly intriguing but little-known aspect of the campaign.
[2] Tim Cook, *Clio's Warriors: Canadian Historians and the Writing of the World War* (Vancouver: UBC Press, 2006), 180.
[3] See, for example, Daniel Dancocks, *The D-Day Dodgers: The Canadians in Italy, 1943-1945* (Toronto: McClelland & Stewart, 1991), and Bill McAndrew, *Canadians and the Italian Campaign* 1943-1945 (Montreal: Art Global, 1996).
[4] By the time of the campaign in Italy, standard British, and consequently Canadian, doctrine had established the composition of armoured divisions at one armoured brigade of three regiments plus an attached motorized infantry battalion, and one infantry brigade. Independent armoured brigades were not permanently attached to divisions, and were composed of three armoured regiments but lacked the motorized infantry battalion, as they existed only to be attached to infantry divisions for combat operations.
[5] C.J.C. Molony, *The Mediterranean and Middle East Volume VI: Victory in the Mediterranean, Part I: 1st April to 4th June 1944* (London: Her Majesty's Stationery Office, 1986), 620; Bill Hartung, ts, n.d., 143rd Infantry, Texas MFM website, 36th ID Assoc, www.kwanah.com/36Division/pstoc, in Rick Atkinson, *The Day of Battle: The War in Sicily and Italy, 1943-1944* (New York: Henry Holt & Co., 2007), 343.
[6] Atkinson, *The Day of Battle*, 349.
[7] War Diary, 1st Canadian Armoured Brigade Headquarters, April 8th 1944.
[8] Dharm Pal, *Official History of the Indian Armed Forces in the Second World War 1939-45: The Campaign in Italy 1945-45* (Calcutta: Sree Saraswaty Press, 1960), 157.
[9] War Diary, 1st Canadian Armoured Brigade Headquarters, April 1944, Appendix 40: *13 Corps - Summary of Corps Commander's Address to Senior Officers of 13 Corps at Venafro, 8th April 44*, 1.

---

[10] These modular bridges, built of steel trusses and panels light enough for parties of engineers to carry and assemble by hand, were developed by the British during the Second World War as a faster means of bridging geographical obstacles, and were instrumental in the Allied advance up the Italian peninsula.
[11] Pal, *The Campaign in Italy 1943-45*, 156; War Diary, Three Rivers Regiment, April 24th 1944.
[12] War Diary, Three Rivers Regiment, May 1st 1944.
[13] War Diary, Three Rivers Regiment, April 1944, Appendix 9: *12 CAR Op Orders,"Special Tk Crew Trg"* (April 26th 1944), 1.
[14] War Diary, Three Rivers Regiment, April 1944, Appendix 15: *21 Inf Bde Op Instructions, "8 Ind Div Planning Notes No. 15* (April 18th 1944), 5; War Diary, Three Rivers Regiment, May 1944, Appendix 16: "17 Ind Inf Bde Operation Order No. 22" (May 9th 1944), 6.
[15] War Diary, Three Rivers Regiment, April 1944, Appendix 15: *21 Inf Bde Op Instructions, "8 Ind Div Planning Notes No. 15* (April 18th 1944), 5.
[16] War Diary, 1st Canadian Armoured Brigade Headquarters, May 1944, Appendix 49 Part One: "19th Ind Inf Bde OO No. 26" (May 9th 1944), 1, 2, 5.
[17] War Diary, Three Rivers Regiment, May 11th 1944.
[18] Nicholson, *The Canadians in Italy 1943-1945*, 399; War Diary, 1st Canadian Armoured Brigade Headquarters, May 1944, Appendix 32: "8 Ind Div Intelligence Summary No. 102" (May 12th 1944), 1.
[19] G.W.L. Nicholson, *Official History of the Canadian Army in the Second World War Volume II: The Canadians in Italy 1943-1945* (Ottawa: Queen's Printer, 1966), 395.
[20] Ibid., 402.
[21] Pal, *The Campaign in Italy 1943-45*, 166.
[22] War Diary, 1st Canadian Armoured Brigade Headquarters, May 1944, Appendix 50: *1 Canadian Armoured Brigade Intelligence Log - "Exercise Honker"* (May 12th 1944), 4.
[23] War Diary, 1st Canadian Armoured Brigade Headquarters, May 1944, Appendix 50: *1 Canadian Armoured Brigade Intelligence Log - "Exercise Honker"* (May 12th 1944), 4; War Diary, 1st Canadian Armoured Brigade Headquarters, May 12th 1944.
[24] "Report on Operations of the 11 CAR from 11 May to 30 May 44", 2. Directorate of History and Heritage, 141.4A11.013 (D1).
[25] War Diary, 1st Canadian Armoured Brigade Headquarters, May 1944, Appendix 50: *1 Canadian Armoured Brigade Intelligence Log - "Exercise Honker"* (May 12th 1944), 6.
[26] Ibid.
[27] "Report on Operations of the 11 CAR from 11 May to 30 May 44", 2. Directorate of History and Heritage, 141.4A11.013 (D1); Nicholson, *The Canadians in Italy*, 403.
[28] War Diary, 1st Canadian Armoured Brigade Headquarters, May 12th 1944; War Diary, The Ontario Regiment, May 12th 1944.

---

[29] War Diary, 1st Canadian Armoured Brigade Headquarters, May 1944, Appendix 50: *1 Canadian Armoured Brigade Intelligence Log - "Exercise Honker"* (May 12th 1944), 7-9.
[30] C.P. Stacey, *The Canadian Army 1939-1945: An Official Historical Summary* (Ottawa: King's Printer, 1948), 135.
[31] Nicholson, *The Canadians in Italy*, 402; Mark Zuehlke, *The Liri Valley: Canada's World War II Breakthrough to Rome* (Toronto: Stoddart, 2001), 115; War Diary, 1st Canadian Armoured Brigade Headquarters, May 12th 1944.
[32] Jim Quinn, "Gari River and the Gustav & Hitler Lines," *Onward II: The Informal History of the Calgary Regiment, 14th Canadian Armoured Regiment*, Dick and Jessie Maltby, eds. (Vancouver: 50/14 Veteran's Association, 1989), n.p., in Zuehlke, *The Liri Valley*, 126.
[33] Pal, *The Campaign in Italy 1943-45*, 170.
[34] Ibid., 169.
[35] War Diary, The Ontario Regiment, May 12th-13th 1944.
[36] War Diary, the Ontario Regiment, May 1944, Appendix 3: *Sitreps for the Month of April* (misfiled): "1 CAB Sitrep May 12th 1944, 1930 hrs"; Pal, *The Campaign in Italy*, 171.
[37] War Diary, 1st Canadian Armoured Brigade Headquarters, May 1944, Appendix 50: *1 Canadian Armoured Brigade Intelligence Log - "Exercise Honker"* (May 12th 1944), 12.
[38] The Highlanders had been so badly mauled by the day's fighting that they were withdrawn over the Gari in the early hours of 13 May to regroup, with the 3rd/8th Punjab Regiment being ordered to continue their aggressive patrolling to guard the southern flank of the bridgehead. Pal, *The Campaign in Italy 1943-45*, 171.
[39] War Diary, The Ontario Regiment, May 1944, Appendix 3: *Sitreps for the Month of April* (misfiled): "1 CAB Sitrep May 12th 1944, 1930 hrs."
[40] War Diary, 1st Canadian Armoured Brigade Headquarters, May 1944, Appendix 32: "8 Ind Div Intelligence Summary No. 102" (May 12th 1944), 1.
[41] Pal, *The Italian Campaign 1943-45*, 172.
[42] Ibid., 173.
[43] War Diary, 1st Canadian Armoured Brigade Headquarters, May 1944, Appendix 50: *1 Canadian Armoured Brigade Intelligence Log - "Exercise Honker"* (May 13th 1944), 8, 11.
[44] "Report on Operations of the 11 CAR from 11 May to 30 May 44", 5. Directorate of History and Heritage, 141.4A11.013 (D1).
[45] War Diary, the Calgary Regiment, May 13th 1944; Pal, *The Italian Campaign 1943-45*, 174.
[46] Pal, *The Italian Campaign 1943-45*, 175.
[47] War Diary, 1st Canadian Armoured Brigade Headquarters, Appendix 50: *1 Canadian Armoured Brigade Intelligence Log - "Exercise Honker"* (May 13th 1944), 6.
[48] Ibid., 12.
[49] Molony, *Victory in the Mediterranean*, 120.

---

50 War Diary, 1st Canadian Armoured Brigade Headquarters, May 1944, Appendix 32: "8 Ind Div Intelligence Summary No. 103" (May 13th 1944), 1.
51 Ibid., 2.
52 War Diary, Three Rivers Regiment, May 14th 1944.
53 War Diary, 1st Canadian Armoured Brigade Headquarters, May 1944, Appendix 50: *1 Canadian Armoured Brigade Intelligence Log - "Exercise Honker"* (May 14th 1944), 13.
54 War Diary, Three Rivers Regiment, May 14th 1944.
55 War Diary, 1st Canadian Armoured Brigade Headquarters, May 1944, Appendix 50: *1 Canadian Armoured Brigade Intelligence Log - "Exercise Honker"* (May 14th 1944), 13.
56 War Diary, 1st Canadian Armoured Brigade Headquarters, May 1944, Appendix 50: *1 Canadian Armoured Brigade Intelligence Log - "Exercise Honker"* (May 14th 1944), 7-8.
57 War Diary, the Ontario Regiment May 14th 1944; Pal, *The Campaign in Italy 1943-45*, 178.
58 Pal, *The Campaign in Italy 1943-45*, 179.
59 War Diary, Three Rivers Regiment, May 1944, Appendix 34: Sitreps, "Last Light Sitrep to 2230 hours 15 May 44."
60 War Diary, the Calgary Regiment, May 15th 1944; Pal, *The Campaign in Italy 1943-45*, 181.
61 Stan Kanik, interview by Mark Zuehlke, Sidney, BC, August 9th 2000, in Zuehlke, *The Liri Valley*, 159.
62 Nicholson, *The Canadians in Italy*, 408.
63 "Report on Operations of the 11 CAR from 11 May to 30 May 44", 7. Directorate of History and Heritage, 141.4A11.013 (D1).
64 War Diary, 1st Canadian Armoured Brigade Headquarters, May 1944, Appendix 1, *Appendix to War Diary*, page 2.

We Survived by Luck, God, Fate and Training: Army Memoires of the Second World War

by
Amanda Shepherd

When the alarm sounded that Canada was going back to war, thousands of Canadian men flocked to enlist. Their thoughts were on finding adventure, honouring their family and country, having a full-time employment; few considered not coming back home. Once they were in combat and facing the possibility of death, soldiers were frequently tormented by questions about survival. Many soldiers believed that there was something helping them survive the perils of the Second World War. It was more than just their abilities that got them through it. God, luck, fate, instincts, and proper training were all primary means of survival for those involved in the Second World War. Army memoires written by the combatants are significant sources to find these themes in. They are an important source for historians to use as they contain the experiences, thoughts, and feelings of those who participated rather than just having the operational papers and diaries to understand the battles. This paper sets to discuss the survival themes of Canadian army memoires from the Second World War. The memoires being examined are from fighting soldiers, officers, and the commanding officers that were on the battlefield with the men. Surviving the war was the primary objective of both the fighting soldiers and commanding officers, whether it was personally surviving the war or the survival of the men. The memoires cover numerous different battles and campaigns from the Dieppe Raid, to the Italian Campaign, to the Normandy Invasion. Each man had a very different war experience and different means of survival and what they believed kept them alive during the war depending on the battle and campaign in which they participated.

Memoires fall under the genre of personal narratives, which also encompass letters and diaries. Many soldiers kept diaries of their experiences and sent letters home during the war. They also used these diaries and letters as references when writing their memoires years later. Soldiers and the families of the soldiers often turned these historical documents into books, so their stories could be heard. Some published their works for their families to record what they did; others, published to add to the historical discussion on the war. Historian Tim Cook asserts that those who control the records control the past.[1] Memoires are a different type of history that do not require archival records (although some authors choose to consult these records to ensure their story is correct). Memoires, as well as war novels, became the history of the masses because they offer a glimpse into the experience of battle that cannot be found in the academic and official histories. Memoires are one man's war, covering a specific period of battle and usually only for a duration of twelve to eighteen months.[2] While these stories offer different perspectives of the war, there is a limited readership to them unless they are a 'hero' or a well-known soldier. As time progressed, more people began reading these stories because they wanted to learn more about the war and these memoires provided a great opportunity to understand the war from the soldier's point of view.

While memoires contain a wealth of information that are not found in official histories, there are some drawbacks to using them for historical research. Memoires are frequently written years after the event took place. Due to this lapse in time, one has to be cautious when using them because this time lapse could dull the accuracy of events which could affect reputations of those involved.[3] Memories may be dulled by time; however, this should not dissuade historians from examining this body of literature. Historians need to be critical of all sources presented to them including memoires. The perspective of the soldiers in combination with the official records and war diaries would create a rounded account that historians could use. The archival record would help fill any gaps within the memoir or correct mistakes. The publishing of these memoires can also be concerning. Many of them are publish in private or small publishing companies that the general population or historians might have difficulties obtaining them.

The literature of Canada's involvement in World War I and II is substantial, with official histories, academic literature, and personal narratives. Memoires of the soldiers who participated in the war started getting published within the first years after the Great War. Even with the participants publishing during and after the war, there were only a small number actually being written. After the second war, there were even fewer memoires being written by the fighting soldiers than that of the Great War.[4] Cook hypothesized that the immediate reasons for this small amount was due to veterans trying to reintegrate back into society; unwillingness to dwell on the past; no market for memoir readership; and the difficulties in talking about war experiences.[5] Many soldiers believed that the average Canadian, during the period after 1918 and again after 1945, was not interested in the terrible trials of the war. However, even with this lack of readership and belief of the lack of interest, soldiers still wrote their stories.[6] Memoires were often cathartic and part of the healing process for the soldiers. Some wrote memoires as a way to start the record straight; others were seeking recognition or trying to document or make sense of their role within a momentous history.[7] There was, for example, a surge of soldier memoires from the Second World War in the 1980s, after the veterans were able to reflect on their lives since the war. Even when the market for military memoires weaned, veterans, their children or grandchildren continued to have the stories published as forms of commemoration, remembrance, and personal fealty.[8] Themes of survival are easily found within the memoires of these veterans.

Survival by luck, God, and fate are found within the fighting soldiers' stories. These terms are often used interchangeably, with similar meaning in the stories. Luck is defined as "success or failure apparently brought by chance than through one's own actions."[9] The soldiers who said that luck was on their side meant that it was good luck keeping them alive, not anything they were doing themselves. Fate is defined as "the development of events outside a person's control, regarded as predetermined by a supernatural power."[10]

Soldiers taking this belief that it was their destiny to stay alive. God is defined as "the creator and ruler of the universe and source of all moral authority; the supreme being."[11] Each of these terms held different meanings to the soldiers who used them. Each soldier named one of these terms in their memoir and attributed it as their means of survival. Soldiers looked towards some higher power or item to hold on to and attributed to their survival. They needed something to hold on to while being in battles. They, often, did not attribute their survival to their training or skills that they acquired during the war. Officers often focused on proper training and education as the means of survival for their men. They believed that if the men were properly trained then they were more likely to survive they battle than if they did not know how to use their weapon or know where they should be located. Luck is also found within the officer's stories when their experiences fighting are being described and not when they were commanding the men.

Surviving the war was the main purpose of Jack Poolton after he was taken prisoner by the Germans following the Dieppe Raid. Luck and near misses helped Poolton survive. Poolton's memoir *Destined to Survive: A Dieppe Veteran's Story* (1998) provides a detailed account of a young solider trying to survive being a prisoner of war (POW) after the Dieppe Raid. He uses the term luck throughout this memoir when describing different situations that he found himself in. Poolton enlisted in 1940 and was posted with the Royal Regiment of Canada. On 19 August 1942, he landed on Puys Beach with the Royal Regiment of Canada. Poolton was lucky to survive the landing and getting onto the beach when so many of his regiment did not. Poolton describes on incident when he was trying to get up the beach: "a sniper hit the rim of my helmet, almost knocking off my head. I was lucky that he did not hit the haversack that contained the 12 two-inch mortar bombs."[12] He had the mortars with him from when he landed and it was luck that the sniper missed the mortars and only hit his helmet. Poolton was lucky to have survived the raid and was not wounded when many of this regiment did not.

Luck was still on Poolton's side after being captured by the Germans. He was placed in the prison camp Stalag VIIIB in Germany.

Escaping was the only thing on Poolton's mind once he was captured. He made one escape attempt and was able to get away for a short time. Poolton was caught again by a local Germans and was lucky that he was not shot during the capture. While being interviewed by the German's, the German said "he was lucky that he had not been shot" and was going back to the prison camp.[13] Luck appeared to keep Poolton from succumbing to the elements during the death march the prisoners were on at the end of the war in 1945. Poolton stated that it was luck that a care package from his cousin arrived the morning of the march and it contained cigarettes that he would be able to use for barter and smoking himself.[14] He was also lucky that his mother sent him extra socks that he could use on the march when the majority of the other men only had one pair that would freeze overnight. He was also very lucky that he wired his drinking mug to his belt so he was able to get drinks whenever he could and would not have to fight with other prisoners for the liquid.[15]

While luck was found throughout Poolton's memoir, near misses or destiny are also found in his tale. The title of his memoir elicits the imaginary that it was his destiny to survive the war and his years as being a prisoner of war. As soon as Poolton was captured at Dieppe, he wanted to escape. He tried once on the train ride to the prison camp; however, the Germans found the hole in the train car before he was able to escape.[16] Once at the camp, Poolton tried to find any way that he could escape. Even after he was recaptured after his escape attempt, he continued to try to get out of the camp and back to his regiment. Poolton's first near miss or destiny stepping in was when he and other prisoners dug a tunnel to escape from. Before Poolton was able to use the tunnel to escaped, they were moved camps. He later found out that another prisoner used that tunnel and was shot by the Germans when he was caught.[17] It could have easily been Poolton; however, this near miss saved his life. The death march was full of near misses for Poolton. He decided that he was going to try escaping again, before he attempted the escape, he went into a barn with some cows to get some milk for his journey. The owner of the barn caught him and tried to attack him. Poolton was able to escape and get back to group. When the farmer went to identify him with the Germans, he was unable to do so.[18] Poolton would have been put to death for that escape attempt had the farmer been able to identify him. This was his last near miss before he was liberated by the Americans.

Luck, similar to Poolton's experience, played a significant role in the experiences of Private Stan Scislowski; however, his memoir also heavily features references to the role he felt that God played within his experiences. In his memoir *Not All of Us Were Brave* (1997), Scislowski states that he was not a hero in the war and most soldiers did not care to be one or cared about getting a medal. They just wanted to survive to get back home. He was drafted into the army in 1943. Scislowski begins the memoir describing, in detail, the training that his regiment received for the first year of service in England. He was sent to Italy in 1944. He believed that the training he received before moving to the front lines was important in keeping alive; however, God and luck also played a significant role.

Scislowski began reaching towards God early on in his war experiences. During one of his first battles, the Battle of the Riccio River, 1944, he began "begging that God would get their asses out of their and quick."[19] Another instance he believed that it was a miracle that no one in his company were hit during a German attack. The Germans had managed to miss his entire company.[20] Scislowski began to believe that God was keeping him and the company safe the more it seemed his prayers were answered by surviving the battles and hardships. He spoke about having a guardian angel that was keeping him alive. He believed he should have been dead more than once; however, his guardian angel kept him alive. During one German attack, he was running in an open field and his company believed that he should have been killed during that attack and they did not know how he survived.[21] By the end of the war, Scislowski fully believed that it was God keeping him and others alive. This is evident during a descriptive passage of a German attack of an Italian village where he prayed asking God to keep the women and children safe during the bombing. This unit was about to open fire on the Germans who were bombing the area, when they noticed a group of civilians trying to escape from the area. Scisloski "never prayed for himself as he fervently as he did for them."[22] He believed it was a miracle that none of the women or children were hurt during that attack. This affirmed Scislowski's believe God was in control of survival.

Scislowski believed that God helped keep him alive; he also believed that luck played a role. His memoir is full of near misses that he attributes to luck. After one of the initial fights, Scislowski was trying to find a place to sleep for the night. The German's had started setting off mortars and they all missed the area he was at. Scislowski believed it was luck that the German aim was off.[23] Another incident he describes where luck was on his side was when he was on guard one night and the thought a group of Germans were trying to get into their area. Something inside him made him hesitate, and then when he went to pull the pin of a grenade, it did not explode. It was luck that he had a dud grenade since it was his own patrol party returning.[24] Scislowski also describes battle luck as a means of keeping him alive during one battle where they had to run through German fire without cover. Scislowski fully believed that God and luck were the two major entities that kept him alive.

While Sciclowski focused on God and luck as the means of survival, George A. Reid's *Speed's War* (2007) focuses on luck and chance. Reid makes no mention of God being the higher power at work. Reid went to Italy and was also captured by the Germans. It was during this time in captivity that luck and chance kept him alive. He states that he wrote the memoir to record his experiences of the war but not to make a hero of himself. He also states that some of the names and places he does not fully remember, however, he recalls the events vividly.[25] Having this stated at the beginning, gives historians or others who read the memoir the understanding that some things in the memoir might not be accurate when referencing other works or official histories.

Reid's memoir is another one of survival attributed to luck and chance. Reid was captured while on patrol with his sergeant.[26] He tried to protect his sergeant by refusing to give any information about him, even when he was getting beaten by the Germans. Reid spent eighteen months in eight different Nazi POW camps. He only remained in Italy a short time before they sent him and other prisoners to Germany. In April 1945, he and a group escaped and found themselves in the hands of the Americans.[27] It was luck that they found the Americans as they had no idea where they were in Germany. The Americans wanted to send them back to their company; however, they ended up getting sent directly back to Canada after their experiences.[28] Reid's story is a true survival. The last paragraph of his memoir sums up the amount of times he almost died and the injuries that he did sustain while being a prisoner and the subsequent escape.[29] Historians are able to get a glimpse into what soldiers endured when captured by the Germans. Reid's story is similar to that of Harry Pope as he was also a POW; however, Reid spent a significant more time in the POW camp.

Instincts and fate assisted Fred Cederberg survive the war. Cederberg's memoir *The Long Road Home: The Autobiography of a Canadian Soldier in Italy in World War II* (1984), provides a detailed account of a soldier's everyday experience in Italy. The majority of the memoir does not spend detailing the battle experiences, but rather the experiences that him and his friends had in Italy. When Cederberg does describe his battle experiences, he often credits his instincts and luck for keeping him alive. During one fire fight, Cederberg describes how he trusted in God and his instincts to keep him alive and able to take over the Bren gun.[30] He had just watched another soldier lose his arm at that gun; however, trusted that he could operate it and nothing would happen to him. During another incident, Cederberg believed that another attack was about to take place and started to get everyone to dig trenches. His instincts told him that they needed to dig these trenches. The trenches saved his life and the others with him.[31] Through the memoir, Cederberg points out that he knew an attack was going to take place before it happened. His trusted his instincts over everything.

Fate is also present in Cederberg's memoir; however, he does not put much faith in the fates for keeping him and the company alive. During one passage he describes the fates as giving them big smiles but they are just waiting to give them the old fickle finger.[32] Another soldier told him not to be so pessimistic and to count the wins and not the losses. This illustrates that Cederberg believed more in his own instincts than of a higher power controlling everything. Even with this lack of belief, near the end of the memoir, Cederberg describes how a shell landed where he was located and it turned out to be a dud. He would have been killed had fate not stepped in.[33]

The next memoir to be discussed moves away from the Italian campaign and goes over to the Normandy invasion in 1944. Continuing the theme of luck as the means of survival, Herbert C. Saunders's *My Story: The War Years* was another memoir where a soldier was lucky to survive a friendly fire attack and a major injury. Saunders enlisted when the call for volunteers came. Saunders's memoir discusses the means of survival in battle, not just against the enemy but also their own military. He describes and incident where his line was being bombed by their own heavy bombers. The bombers mistook them for the enemy line. Saunders survived this friendly attack while one was killed and four others were wounded.[34] He believed that luck played a role in his survival.

Saunders went into France just after the initial Normandy invasion. He helped with the containment and pushing of the line. He was quickly sent to Belgium then to Holland. He describes the most important moment of his survival. While on patrol, Saunders stepped on a landmine and it blew up. He lost his right foot in the blast. However, he survived it.[35] He attributed this to luck that he only lost his foot and not his life. Due to his injury, he was sent back to England and then Canada to heal.

While his memoir is short and contains numerous pictures and explanatory appendices, his memoir still offers a different perspective of this role in the war. His case is the only out of the memoires discussed where an injury forced the end of his military career. In his postscript, he attributes luck to his survival of the war but also that good planning from the officers kept him alive.

While soldiers often credited luck, fate, and God as the means of survival, officers had a different view of what would keep their men alive. Luck and God did not have a place, rather proper training and education would ensure that the men would survive. Howard Graham's *Citizen and Soldier: The Memoires of Lieutenant-General Howard Graham* (1987) memoir encompasses Graham's experiences during First World War, the interwar period, and Second World War. His experiences differ from the memoires thus examined as he served every rank in the service through his career, from private to lieutenant-general.[36] The theme of survival is found in Graham's memoir, as he spent the First World War trying to survive and the Second World War trying to keep the men he commanded alive.[37]

During the First World War, Graham enlisted once he turned eighteen. His mother went to the Colonel in their town to get him a non-combat position within the army. However, the army sent the soldiers where they were needed and could not ensure that they would stay at a non-combat position.[38] Graham describes various battles and trench warfare. He mentions the Battle of Vimy Ridge and Passchendaele; however, goes into more detail of the battle of Amiens in 1918 and states that the battle was just as important as the other two were.[39] He was wounded while fighting in the trenches and was sent back to headquarters until he was fit for duty again. It was luck that he was able to get sent back to headquarters again rather than being sent back to the front after his wounds healed. He believed that he was just in the right place at the right time to being sent to headquarters. Graham's experience in the war differs slightly because while he was working in headquarters he was privy to information that most of soldiers of his rank would not have.[40] It also differs from the typical fighting soldiers' experience because of the significant amount of time spent at headquarters instead of being at the front with the rest of the men.

Graham's war experience in the Second World War was starkly different than his experience in the First World War. This is evident when he describes his feeling when he received the information that his regiment was being mobilized.[41] There was also a different perspective of this war compared to the pervious. There was little enthusiasm for the war in 1939 and "the cause" that had been present in 1914.[42] This shows the first shift in perspectives of war. Graham was passed over early for the command of his unit. While disappointed, he was also relieved as he was concerned for the welfare of the troops and believed they were not ready for battle.[43] He was promoted to lieutenant-colonel and commander of his unit on 2 September, 1940. Shortly after Graham took command of his unit, he was issues orders that everyone needed to be prepared for an immediate attack from the Germans. He went to each company to ensure that they were prepared and stayed prepared.[44] Graham spent a great deal of time running different exercises for his men to ensure that they were battle ready. The reader can get a sense of the sincerity that Graham felt for his troops when he was given command of another brigade.

Graham's new command took him to Italy. Before going to Italy, his new brigade went through vigorous training for this new campaign. He wanted to make sure that his troops were ready to fight in all conditions once they arrived in Italy. Graham believed that every soldier should know why they had to go through certain types of training or follow certain orders. He wanted them to understand the rationale behind the orders.[45] Graham and his brigade landed in Italy in July of 1943. Once ashore, he did whatever he needed to do in order to keep his men alive. Early in the campaign, Graham had to send his brigade through an enemy stronghold outside the town of Valguarnera. He made sure to gather as much information from the previous brigade that tried to take the area to ensure that he did not have the same amount of casualties. He made sure that his men were prepared and ready for the battle.[46] Graham continued to do everything that he could to keep his men alive during this campaign. He stayed with his brigade until a medical condition required him to be sent bacl to England in early 1944. Graham's First World War experiences shaped how he led his men during the Italian Campaign and ensured that his men survived.

Lieutenant- General E. L. M. Burns follows suit with Graham concluding that proper training and education would ensure the survival of the men they were in charge of. His memoir *General Mud: Memories of Two World Wars* (1970) also covers both wars. In his introduction, Burns describes some of the challenges of writing a memoir and using it for historical reference. He states that it was difficult remembering fifty years back in order to give the vivid details of the sights and smells of the war and that memoires may suffer from faulty memory, bias, or untruths.[47] These are all items that historians need to be aware of when using memoires as sources as Burns was aware. Burns also hoped to fill a gap in the Canadian memoir literature—no Canadian generals had written them.[48] He used his regiment's war diaries for references, and makes references to other outside sources and contains numerous footnotes for each chapter.

Burns fought in both world wars and his memoir focuses on the major battles and the actions of the commanders. He focuses heavily on the Battles of the Somme and Vimy Ridge in his narrative of the First World War.[49] He believed that these victories were based on effective planning of the commanders and the skills of the soldier who followed the orders. He also believed that the loss of leaders was the most series in battle as they were the ones who knew what was taking place.[50]

The theme of survival is found within Burns's narrative. He described failures of the soldiers not being trained properly would lead to them getting killed.[51] Burns's First World War experience helped him command in the Second World War.[52] He provides numerous examples of how the past war shaped the current one. Properly trained men and weapons were two skills that Burns pushed for. When he took command of an armoured unit in 1941, he went about trying to make sure his men were training properly. This proved to be difficult; there were not enough supplies for the men to use for training. Burns wanted to make sure that the men were trained properly to survive facing the Germans.[53] Burns often remembered the Battle of Vimy Ridge when he was trying to get the men ready for battle: "I aimed to ensure that no men should go into battle without knowing how to use their weapons."[54] He would not let reinforcement men into battle until he saw that they could fire a weapon properly. Certain failures from the first war came out again, in the Italian campaign of which Burns was a part. However, they were quickly corrected before they could happen again. He ends his narrative with stating that Canadians should not forget the valor of soldiers who fought and war the Italian campaign and the sacrifices that were made.[55]

Planning and training were mechanisms of survival for the men under the command of Major-General Kitching. The memoir *Mud and Green Fields: The Memoires of Major-General George Kitching* (1993) was written by a veteran of both the Italian and Normandy campaign. The Foreword, written by historian Colonel Charles P. Stacey, states that Kitching rose through the ranks in the army, similar to Graham's experience, and was involved in most of the theatres that they Canadian army had fought in.[56] His narrative includes his early days in China, his schooling in England, and his early military career in the British army. It is during the Second World War that Kitching took a command in the Canadian army. The memoir is battle heavy once he begins describing his experiences during the war. There is significant tactical information discussed and later politics after the war.

The Italian Campaign is often overshadowed by other campaigns, but Kitching believed that it was the finest hour for the allies.[57] Planning was an important aspect of the victory. The plans were sound and sensible. Command examined ways to ensure their men would survive the campaign. Unlike Burns, Kitching spent the majority of his command in headquarters rather than on the lines with his men. However, he made sure that the plans for his soldiers were solid before following them. Kitching was able to attend the meetings that produced the German surrender of the war.[58] This is a unique experience and is only found in this narrative in this study. This gives the reader an interesting view on how a war is actually ended and not just the ending of fighting.

Harry Pope, while did not hold a commanding officer role was still an officer in the military, focuses on the training and education he received to survive being captured and his subsequent escape. Pope was another soldier who was a part of the Italian campaign. His memoir *Leading From the Front: The War Memoires of Harry Pope* (2002) describes his experiences in the Second World War and the Korean War. Pope states that he wrote his memoir for soldiers who had not been to war and wanted others learn from the mistakes that he made in hopes that they would not be repeated.[59] Pope's memoir is one of survival. During his time in the Italian campaign, he was taken prisoner by the Germans and spent two months trying to get back to his men. Pope focuses on the training that he received as the means for his survival not chance or luck.

Pope was sent to Italy with the Quebec "Van Doos."[60] He often questioned the orders of his commanding officer because the officers were too far from the battle lines to make proper decisions. He vowed that he would not make these mistakes and would take as few of risks as possible with the lives of his men. He wanted to ensure the survival of his men and not see a waste of their lives. In May 1944, Pope was captured by the Germans while collecting his company's wounded.[61] Pope described how he was captured after getting one of his men killed another badly wounded and then his men taken as prisoners. However, he did not see this as dishonourable.[62] When first captured, he fought with the Germans over being taken prisoner, as he was wearing a Red Cross arm band and they did not have a right to take him and his men.[63] Even in war, there are rules that needed to be followed and Pope fought for them. Pope was sent to a POW camp where he was able to escape during a fifty-mile march. He spent the next month surviving being behind enemy lines and trying to get back to his men.[64] Pope focused on his military training to keep him safe while he was behind enemy lines.[65] This memoir gives an interesting perspective, as few officers who were captured were able to escape and wrote their experiences about it. After his escape, Pope continued to fight in the war with his men. He was later transferred to be under the command of Burns.

Proper training and education and luck were a common theme found in Farley Mowat's memoir *And No Birds Sang* (2012). Mowat provided vivid descriptions of his experiences in the Italian campaign with Able Company. He went overseas in 1942 as a 2nd lieutenant. Mowat focuses his memoir not on the battle tactics of war but rather the individual experiences he had with his men. At the beginning of the memoir, he focuses on the training he received before going into battle. During one fire fight with the Germans, he was delighted to discover that he could identify most of the German weapons.[66] Mowat had spent a significant amount of time studying the weapons and could tell his men what to expect with each weapon firing. He also believed that officers needed to have the proper training for battles, not just the fighting soldiers. He describes how after their sergeant-major was killed, another officer began giving orders in a formal manner that were prescribed in the military textbooks which seemed incomprehensible.[67] This illustrated that officers needed to be battle ready from knowing how to properly use a weapon to properly give orders that soldiers will understand.

Mowat contents that luck kept him alive during the war. He describes numerous near death experiences that he attributes to luck for him staying alive and keeping his men alive. During one instance, Mowat describes how he was almost run over by a truck when the truck hit a Teller mine. He believed that luck kept him alive and uninjured when two others were killed and seven were wounded. The truck was carrying mortar bombs that should have exploded when it hit the mine, but they did not.[68] During one skirmish with the Germans, Mowat accidently shot a red flare where he was. The Germans started firing in that direction and he screamed for his platoon to get out of the area. He describes that "it was every man for himself, but luck was with us for every man made it over the crest..."[69] Within the memoir, Mowat included numerous letters that he wrote home. After winning the battle of Grammichele, he wrote a letter to a friend home talking about the battle and luck: "it was exciting as hell, and I didn't lose a single man, though I guess this kind of luck can't last forever."[70] He understood that luck was not always going to be around him. At some point, his luck would run out. In another one of those letters, Mowat describes his thoughts on death during the war and soldiers always looking for Lady Luck:

Dying is just a word until you find out differently. That's trite, but horribly true. The first times you almost get nicked you take for granted you are naturally immortal. The next few times you begin to wonder. After that you start looking over your soldier to make sure old Lady Luck is still around.[71]

There are various other examples of him believing luck kept him alive, including when he was injured in battle.[72]

While he generally attributed luck to his survival, he believed that God's hand played a role. During one evening movement, Mowat was not sure how his unit was going to accomplish their task because they had numerous obstacles ahead of them. Somehow they accomplished part of their task and he says that God helped them.[73] In another instance, he was thanking God he was injured so he could go home; however, upon examination he found that he was not injured after all.[74] He would often thank God for keeping his men safe, or not seriously injured, coming out of a battle, or not being involved in a bad battle. Mowat describes how he was supposed to be involved in one particular battle, which turned into a bad battle, however, he ended up getting sick and did not participate. He believed that God did not want him in that battle. When he went back to the front to see what happened at the battle, all he could do was thank God that he was not there. So many of the men were killed and he knew that he easily could have been one.[75]

The perspectives found in the memoires examined all shape how the Canadian involvement in the Second World War is remembered. Each soldier, officer, or other ranks, had very different experiences to the war. The main theme found in all the memoires was one of survival. Each of the commanding officers had the responsibility of keeping their troops alive as well as providing victories through the battles. As shown through the memoires, some officers took the means of survival of their men as more of a priority than others. Officers focused on having their soldiers properly trained and educated to keep them alive, while soldiers believed God, luck, fate and instincts were the means of survival. By attributing survival to these terms, soldiers believed that survival was not something that they were responsible for but rather it was a higher power or their destiny that was running the show. Burns' wanted his experiences from the First World War to help make him a better commander during the second war. Pope saw the mistakes that other officers were making and wanted to ensure that he learned from them in order to save the lives of his men. The fighting soldiers just wanted to get back to their families and held onto the hope by attributing their survival to luck, fate, and God. Historians should not be wary of using memoires as a source of information. The fact that time lapse and the unreliability of memory does mean that we must take these narratives in context (using them as source material for work of a more qualitative nature); however, they are a wealth of information and serve as an excellent complement (and sometimes overlap) to that which is found in the official documents in the archives.

Endnotes

[1] Tim Cook, *Clio's Warriors: Canadian Historians and the Writing of the World Wars*. Toronto: UBC Press, 2006, p. 7.
[2] Cook, p. 46.
[3] Cook, p. 51.
[4] Cook, p. 190.
[5] Cook, p. 74.
[6] Cook, p. 75.
[7] Cook, p. 75.
[8] Cook, p. 241.
[9] *Oxford dictionary*,"luck," accessed March 25, 2018, https://en.oxforddictionaries.com/definition/luck
[10] *Oxford dictionary*, "fate," accessed March 25, 2018, https://en.oxforddictionaries.com/definition/fate
[11] *Oxford dictionary*, "god," accessed March 25, 2018, https://en.oxforddictionaries.com/definition/god
[12] Poolton, Jack A. *Destined to Survive: a Dieppe Veteran's Story*. Toronto: Dundurn Press, 1998, p. 39
[13] Poolton, p. 79.
[14] Poolton, p. 103.
[15] Poolton, p. 105.
[16] Poolton, p. 52.
[17] Poolton, p. 90.
[18] Poolton, p. 108-109.
[19] Stan Scislowski, *Not All of Us Were Brave*, Toronto: Dundurn, 1997, p. 119.
[20] Scislowski, p. 121.
[21] Scislowski, p. 152.
[22] Scislowski, p. 345.
[23] Scislowski, p. 110.
[24] Scislowski, p. 141-142.
[25] George A Reid, *Speed's War: A Canadian Soldier's Memoir of World War II*. Royston: Madrona Books & Publishing, 2007, p. xi.
[26] Reid, p. 33.
[27] Reid, p. 81.
[28] Reid, p. 87.
[29] Reid, p. 93.
[30] Fred Cederberg, *The Long Road Home: The Autobiography of a Canadian Solider in Italy in World War II*. Toronto: General Publishing, 1984, p. 93.
[31] Cederberg, p. 159.
[32] Cederberg, p. 123.
[33] Cederberg, p. 252.
[34] Herbert C. Saunders, *My Story: The War Years*. Victoria: Chaucer Workshop Publishing, 2006, p. 26.
[35] Saunders, p. 59.

---

[36] Howard Graham, *Citizen and Soldier: The Memoires of Lieutenant General Howard Graham*. Toronto: McClelland and Stewart, 1987, p. 55.
[37] Graham took numerous courses to qualify as an officer. He was promoted to the rank of Lieutenant before the second war broke out.
[38] Graham, p. 50. He did not spend as much time on the front lines as most soldiers did. One could credit his mother as the primary reason he came back from the war.
[39] Graham, p. 65.
[40] This information included information about military strength and divisions, and secret counterattacks that would be taking place. Graham, p. 63.
[41] The first war he could not wait to enlist as soon as he turned of age. This war, he hated the thoughts of leaving his wife and child, as well as the life that he built. He also states that he was under no legal obligations to serve outside of Canada; however, believed it would be morally wrong and disloyal not to go. Graham, p. 108.
[42] Graham, p. 109.
[43] Graham, p. 113.
[44] Graham, p. 123.
[45] Grham, p. 137
[46] Graham, p. 165.
[47] E. L. M. Burns, *General Mud: Memoires of Two World Wars.* Toronto: Clarke, Irwin & Company, 1970, p. xi.
[48] At the time of his writing, no Canadian general of the Great War had written their memoires. More generals of the Second World War wrote theirs.
[49] Burns' states that Canadians who fought in WWI took more pride in the conquest of Vimy Ridge than in any other of their battles in the four long and bloody years. Vimy stands out the most. P. 32.
[50] Burns, p. 41.
[51] Burns, p. 77.
[52] Burns states that many veteran commanders from the first war were commanding in the second war aside most did not stay in the command for long. This was a different kind of war and they did not have the ability to command in it.
[53] Burns, p. 110.
[54] Burns, p. 117.
[55] Burns, p. 225.
[56] George Kitching, *Mud and Green Fields: The Memoires of Major-General George Kitching*. St. Catharines: Vanwell Publishing Limited, 1993, p. v.
[57] Kitching, p. 144.
[58] Kitching, p. 226.
[59] Harry Pope, *Leading from the Front: The War Memoires of Harry Pope.* Waterloo: Laurier Centre for Military, Strategic, and Disarmament Studies, Wilfrid Laurier University, 2002, p. ix.
[60] Pope, p. 10

[61] Pope, p. 14.
[62] Pope, p. 18.
[63] Pope, p. 17.
[64] Pope, p. 25-40.
[65] Pope, p. 32.
[66] Mowat, *And No Birds Sang*, Toronto: Douglas & McIntyre, 2012, p. 86.
[67] Mowat, p. 64.
[68] Mowat, p.157-158 .
[69] Mowat, p. 105-106.
[70] Mowat, p. 90
[71] Mowat, p. 186.
[72] See Mowat, p. 209-210.
[73] Mowat, p. 97.
[74] Mowat, p. 210.
[75] Mowat, p. 132.

Leadership and Operational Stress Injuries (OSIs) in the Canadian Army

by

Lieutenant Colonel W.A. (Bill) Leavey MA, CD (Retired)

Success is not final, failure is not fatal:
it is the courage to continue that counts.
Winston Churchill
"Adapt, improvise, overcome." - *'Heart Break Hill'.*
Clint Eastwood as Gunny Highway - US Marines
'HUA' Heard, Understood, Accepted - US Marines

1.0 Introduction

In recent times, the Canadian Forces (CF) has experienced a tsunami of Operational Stress Injuries (OSIs) after our troops experienced brutal combat against terrorist groups in Afghanistan, Iraq, Iran, and Syria; peace-making operations such as Somalia, Rwanda, the former Yugoslavia (Bosnia-Herzegovina, Kosovo and Sarajevo), and Libya; and even humanitarian assistance such as the downed Swiss Air Flight 111 off the coast of Nova Scotia and assistance to Haiti after the devastating earthquake. We as leaders in the CF have been granted the honour and the privilege to command and look after our most valuable commodity, our soldiers. We should be proud of this sacred opportunity, and we must honour it to the very utmost of our abilities, both individually and collectively.

2.0. Background

In the 1990s, after the fall of the Berlin Wall and the disintegration of the Soviet Union, the Cold War, which had occupied the Western Allies for over forty years, ended. The jubilation and Cold War dividends that followed were short lived as countries across the globe began internecine struggles that drew in the major powers. The Canadian Forces (CF) was not immune to this and soon got embroiled in UN, NATO, and Coalition Force operations encompassing peace keeping and peace-making missions in the former Yugoslavia, the Middle East, Far East, Africa, and most recently the NATO show of force operations in the Ukraine and Latvia. Operational tempo increased exponentially with each new tasking as the CF, the Army in particular, became stretched to the limit. Eventually and inevitably the stress and pressure of what became back-to-back overseas tours took its toll on soldiers and their families. Also, the men and women left behind to 'hold the fort' with reduced personnel and resources, were burning out, in high numbers, from fatigue and exhaustion, which bred anxiety, depression, and other mental health (MH) problems at an increasing and distressing rate; leading in too many cases to suicide.

As the dead and wounded repatriated back to Canada, psychological injuries began to appear in alarming numbers. It was a serious crisis. The plague in question was operational stress injuries or (OSIs). A system to help them had to be found. At around the same time, a navy veteran expressed another telling analogy: "When you navigate through fog into unknown territory," the old salt opined, "you go by your wake, where you have already traveled." His metaphor was prescient, as soldiers were haunted by the memory and recurring nightmares of the sights and sounds and smells of the horror and malignancy of the genocides and cruel and brutal atrocities that they witnessed which tortured and tormented their minds.

Their symptoms were many and varied: they could not sleep, they could not eat, and they were overwhelmed by a constant pall of anxiety and hyper-vigilance that enshrouded them. In a futile attempt to hide this, many immersed themselves in work and/or mega-fitness programs, and they refused to admit they were affected by the often-severe stress and horror that they had experienced. The stress and anxiety that followed them home and was now affecting their friends, work mates, and families.

By fabrication, disingenuous response, and rationalization, many convinced themselves, their peers, along with their superiors and the medical system that they were healthy; there was nothing wrong with them, and they didn't need any help especially from a hierarchy and medical system which they did not entirely trust. Later, it was confirmed that many were suffering from what was commonly known as Post Traumatic Stress Disorder (PTSD), a term coined by the Americans after Vietnam in 1980.

A cursory study of the term reveals that it has always been with us; Homer in his heroic epic poem *The Odyssey* wrote about the adventures and hardships of Odysseus (Latin Ulysses) the king of Ithaca and wisest and shrewdest of the Greek leaders during the Trojan War. He described, in detail, the privations and hardships suffered by Odysseus and his crew on their perilous ten-year journey back home to Ithaca by sea. Many of the crewmen, including Odysseus himself, showed serious symptoms of PTSD. Even the ancient Macedonians, Alexander the Great's troops, who were mostly successful, called it 'battle fatigue' when the soldiers were "stricken dumb with terror and had no heart for the fight."

Tolstoy's 1869 masterpiece War and Peace was one of the first historical epic novels to depict the reality of war of the soldiers on the battlefield, the commanders and the affected civilians. It clearly shows the confusion, desperation and futility of war. The novel mixes philosophy, history and fiction in over half a million words deploying several hundred characters and interwoven stories in forensic detail of Russia's struggle with Napoleon from 1805-1814. Tolstoy focuses not only on the war, but the effect on the home front, which transforms the lives of the central characters. Cases of PTSD from the trauma of the conflict are evident throughout the book.

Steven Crane, a young American Civil War correspondent penned *the Thin Red Line,* an iconic American Civil War novel describing the effect of battle stress on Civil War soldiers and introducing the concept of PTSD to millions of readers. During the Civil War it was called 'soldier's heart' because blood pressure and heartbeat increased; they also called extreme homesickness, which took its toll, 'nostalgia.' In the First World War it was dubbed 'shell shock' when the concussion of shelling was blamed. The Russians called it 'battle shock.' And in the Second World War, it was coined as 'battle fatigue.' Other OSIs, including depression, anxiety, and substance abuse, were more prevalent but less damaging and dangerous—it appeared.

During this period, to try to help, and educate all ranks, the CF produced and directed a video on the subject called *Witness the Evil,* which was launched in the fall of 1998 to critical acclaim. All Canadian military personnel would profit from viewing it. Also, in 2014, a video entitled *Soldier' Children—The Voices of Children in Military Families Living with Post Traumatic Stress Disorder* was produced and has given many families suffering from the effects of PTSD hope and healing methods, along with the knowledge that they are not alone.

Some took the situation seriously, but many did not. As an example, around the same time, it was learned that veterans with diagnosed OSIs had been caught playing poker with their pills in the barracks on a Canadian base and one had gone home and overdosed. This added new urgency to the state of affairs; something had to be done soon.

Fledgling programs such as Operational Stress Injury Social Support (OSISS), a peer support program, advanced tentatively, on wobbly legs as the 'OSISS Project.' OSISS is a critical non-clinical addition to the mental health (MH) services in the CF. Shortly after, the Joint Speakers Bureau (JSB) was developed as a separate entity to educate the troops and the chain of command on how to recognize, treat and mitigate OSIs. It was also designed to reduce the stigma on mental health (MH) endured by many of the stricken.

The code of ethics or set of moral principles for the OSISS Program outlines its modus operendi, which is to follow OSISS boundaries and maintain self-care regimens. This includes promoting trust in OSISS collective works and initiatives; respecting the oath of confidentiality and the choices of others; and to use the power differential that fosters empowerment of all Peers. The success of the program has depended substantially on leadership at all levels in the chain of command, from the CDS (Chief of the Defence Staff) down to the most junior corporal.

3.0. Understanding the Causes and Manifestations of OSIs

As with most other things in life, the basic understanding of OSIs lies within the pendulum of cause and effect. A cause is what brings about the problem (OSI) to begin with. An effect is how the OSI manifests itself within the afflicted individual. The causes of OSIs are many and varied.

3.1. Causes

According to Mental Health First Aid Canada, Operational Stress Injuries have four different possible mechanisms or causes.[1] He first of these is trauma, when an individual experiences one or more life-threatening situations, provoking terror, horror, or helplessness. The second is fatigue, when, due to the wear and tear of prolonged stress, including from non-operational sources, the afflicted individual goes without sufficient sleep, rest, and restoration. Although there may not be a single provoking event such as a firefight, the psychological injury is just as real as one from trauma. The third cause of OSIs is grief. Not only does a soldier have to face the deaths of comrades-in-arms, friends, and leaders, but also the strain of long-term separation from loved ones in the civilian world, broken relationships, and family losses. The fourth cause of OSIs is moral injury, which is the violation or disruption of value and belief systems by wrong or inconsistent action or inaction. Soldiers are asked to do things that go against what we understand the laws of nature and morality to be. An example of moral injury is at Appendix A. All of these OSIs can cause tremendous psychological suffering. Leaders, both military and civilian are duty bound to recognize and mitigate OSIs.

3.2. Effects

Crisis leads to stress and stress leads to fear and fear in turn leads to anxiety. Anxiety is the first manifestation of all OSIs and can be caused by trauma, fatigue and other factors listed below. This can propagate into addictions with alcohol and drugs to self medicate, which develops addictions and ultimately violent behaviour including suicide and homicide. In short, it is a vicious circle that causes havoc for soldiers in action. It is our job as leaders to recognize the symptoms and try to mitigate the effects.

3.2.1. Crisis

Although crisis is not the only cause of mental health problems, crisis, by its very nature, manifests OSIs. During periods of crisis leaders must be constantly vigilant for signs and symptoms of stress injuries. When OSIs strike our troops, early detection and prompt remedial action are critical to recovery. The first and most important thing that leaders can do is recognize the symptoms of those suffering from OSIs. Leaders must watch for changes in usual behavior patterns. The CF Principles of Leadership state that leaders must *"Know your soldiers and promote their welfare."* The second step in the order of priority is to quickly get them to the best help and treatment available. These steps can only be accomplished if leaders are constantly vigilant and trained to *"maintain situational awareness: seek information; keep current."*

Leaders need to refer their vulnerable troops to professional available assistance, including medical and psychiatric support personnel. It is far better to make that referral than to have regrets after the individual's condition has worsened or the individual has committed a devastating and permanent act of homicide or suicide.

Crisis is an emotional upset that occurs during a time of danger, severe stress, anxious waiting, and/or disconcerting disappointment. It can be caused by an unexpected event such as the death of a loved one, the loss of a comrade, or a serious life-threatening injury or illness in you or someone close to you. Witnessing the atrocities of ethnic cleansing or handling mass casualties, especially when women, children and the elderly are victims, can cause serious crisis and the accompanying high levels of stress. More pedestrian, but no less damaging, the loss of a coveted job or sought-after appointment, or even more common, the cumulative pressures at home and/ or work can also lead to crisis; and all ranks from private to general are susceptible to the plague of this equal-opportunity condition which lurks in all of our minds.

Crisis can cause negative reactions in anyone regardless of rank or position. Serious contributing factors to crisis in the Canadian Forces (CF) today include the combined effects of increased op tempo and time away from home base for training and courses. This invariably leads to family conflict where alienation, estrangement and even divorce are the inevitable consequences. In these crises, affected individuals may feel alone, helpless and unable to cope. Good leadership; early intervention; access to good resources; and a supportive network of peers, family, and extended family can go a long way towards relieving the consequences of crisis.

Crisis forces the onset of many emotions such as fear, grief, guilt, and anger, which can feel confusing and overwhelming. The combined stress of family, home and work can become unbearable. Exhibiting one or more of the following reactions should act as a warning signal to leaders and followers alike. Patterns of eating and sleeping change, and the individual has difficulty performing normal tasks. This can be accompanied by intense anger and feeling out of control, fearful, and alone, along with guilt and restlessness. Any of these feelings can lead to self-medication with alcohol or drugs to numb the pain.

3.2.2. Stress

The dictionary defines stress as "a force or system of forces that tends to produce deformation in a body." Stress is also described as "an emotional or intellectual strain or tension." Therefore, both physical and psychological injuries (OSIs) are caused by stress._Cumulative stress includes a combination of home/family and job/work stresses which can build up into an overwhelming insurmountable pressure, causing serious and severe mental disorders.

Although closely related, and often considered synonymous, stress and crisis are not the same thing. A crisis is an event; stress is a negative reaction to one or more events. A crisis is always accompanied by stress, but stress does not always create a crisis. Each person views crisis and the inevitable accompanying stressors in his or her own way. Experiencing crisis, particularly prolonged, chronic and cumulative crisis, can be debilitating. Stress can be good and bad; it can be single incident or cumulative and includes both family and work and social stress. At Appendix B, the Holmes-Rahe Stress Evaluation lists a compilation of all stress events and their relative effects on individuals. This reinforces the need for leaders to know what is going on in their men's personal lives. Another principle of leadership, "Know your soldiers and promote their welfare" gives guidance for situations that may place them at risk for mental difficulties. Good leadership resulting in the accompanying high morale and unit cohesion will help to create resilience to crises.

Resilience is the capability of "recoiling from shock or pressure unchanged and undamaged." Resilience produces a hardiness to stress and can make bouncing back from the harmful effects of crisis more likely. As leaders, we are responsible for developing this resiliency in both ourselves and our followers.

Stress and fear are closely related, and they feed off each other. Stress causes fear and fear causes stress. It's a vicious circle which if not interjected will quickly cause serious difficulties in both leaders and rank and file. The key is early recognition of symptoms followed by early intervention to mitigate the physical and psychological manifestations of the resulting OSIs. A WW2 soldier describes stress and fear thusly:

> War is, by far, the most stressful of all human endeavors. Not far behind is the activity of preparing for war. The anticipation of death and dismemberment are constant companions. According to Charles R. Figley, Ph.D., a former U.S. Marine and William P. Nash M.D., a senior U.S. Navy Psychiatrist in their well-researched, widely read *COMBAT Stress Injury,* the strains of battle can be both intense for short periods and cumulative over an extended period. Each, or both in combination, can be devastating as well as debilitating.[2]

Stress and fear did different things to different people, and they all had their own way of coping. Shelling became the constant curse of front-line soldiers. Artillery and mortars were responsible for more casualties on both sides than any other weapons system. John English in his *On Infantry* explains that in "World War II artillery shells accounted for 60 percent of casualties."[3] That's something to be afraid of.

Specifically, the German Nebelwurfer was an electrically detonated type of rocket launcher, with six stove-pipe like barrels. It was dubbed the 'moaning Minnie,' and, according to John Mimms in his hilarious *Spam Medal Heroes,* it was a particularly diabolical invention[4]

Explosives are an unavoidable part of modern soldiering. Ever since the invention of gun powder by the Chinese, combatants have attempted to discover bigger, faster, more effective ways of blowing one another up. While munitions are a major source of stress (particularly to the recipient), most soldiers are fascinated by things that go bang in the night especially if they are setting them off.

3.2.3. Fear

'Nervous in the Service' is a flippant saying describing the anxiety and angst experienced by soldiers in combat or training for combat. Fear is a soldier's worst enemy, and courage is not a lack of fear, but continuing to do our job, despite fear. Fear can also be contagious and destructive, poison in combat. Often, fear of the unknown is the worst. *Leading People* states in part that:

> [T]today's battlespace—the place where operations are conducted and where combat is an ever-present menace and implicit threat—is complex, difficult and dangerous. CF leaders must be prepared to lead in times of uncertainty, ambiguity, confusion, and danger—and above all, fear.[5]

Fear is defined in the dictionary as "an agitated feeling aroused by actual or threatening danger, trouble etc.; dread; terror. The possibility that something dreaded or unwanted may occur." [6] All people experience fear; fear is a powerful emotion that if not checked can debilitate, and paralyze individuals, teams and even whole units. Fear frequently leads to panic and can easily become contagious. Fear can be controlled and used to benefit the military team in times of crisis, danger and stress. The leader's challenge is to understand fear and cope with it. Certain conditions cause specific fears: fear of being killed, wounded or captured; fear of killing others; fear of personal failure and letting comrades down; and probably most prevalent and debilitating, fear of the unknown.

Fatigue, noise, and deprivation aggravate fear. Courage is often touted as the antidote for fear, but leaders must understand that courage is not fearlessness. Courage is being able to work through the fear to get the job done. Education and training, along with high morale, are key to preventing debilitating fear. Also critical are discipline and the development of self-discipline in leaders and followers alike. Physical fitness and mental indoctrination can moderate the impact of fatigue, deprivation and hopelessness. They also improve resilience to stress, build self-confidence and enhance clear thinking during periods of mental fatigue and exhaustion, and the accompanying confusion.

According to a special section entitled FEAR in the Buddhist Review, *Tricycle,* fear has several different components:[7]

> Early in life, we all learn to be afraid of anything that causes us pain. This is an effective way to create the conditions for well-being and safety. The useful kind of fear prepares us to take appropriate action to reduce harm. The other kind, let's call it bad fear, makes us see a snake where a rope has cast a shadow.

Fear is a defence mechanism; we are alerted to a knowable and imminent threat; fear warns our body and nervous system of approaching danger. Anxiety is the reaction to an inner conflict or future threat. It is a dreaded feeling that something unknown and unwanted, beyond one's control, is going to happen.

When we feel fear, we have either an active or passive response. It is either a fight-or-flight reaction or the opposite reaction of freeze or faint. When most people experience acute fear, the blood flows from the brain to the limbs and the mind gets fuzzy; just when we need our thinking to be clear. However, if the nervous system is trained to recover, we're more able to keep calm, breathe, and plan and act.

There are teachings and practices that can be used to reduce and even eliminate the grip of fear. Edith Eva Eger, a clinical psychologist in California, and a survivor of Auschwitz during the holocaust, discusses fear in the tapestry of terror in the concentration camp. The Nazis were institutionally sadistic and brutal in their treatment of the Jewish captives. "During my time in captivity" she writes, "confronting fear and taking action helped me fight off the numbness that persistent contact with arbitrary authority can create. Learning to face fear and realize that you are a human being and have your own thoughts of hope, became an effective technique to recapture self-esteem—one I share with my patients."[8]

Another author, David Brazier in his essay *The Gift of Fear* is convinced that "fear is part of human nature, so there is little point in forcing ourselves to overcome it or pretending to be unaffected by it. In fact, we do so at our peril."[9] H e goes on to say that "Fear is a given; it is a fundamental part of life and consciousness. And while it may not feel good, fear is useful and necessary." A short story further illustrates this concept:

> There was a monastery in the mountains in China. Wild deer would come onto the monastery's beautiful grounds. The monks loved the deer and enjoyed feeding them. When the abbot heard about it, he came out shouting and waving his arms and attacking the deer with his staff. The deer became alarmed and ran away. The abbot put up a notice saying there must be no more feeding of the deer and any deer seen on the property were to be chased off. The monks protested saying, "We came here to learn kindness and compassion. What sort of example are you, getting so mad at these gentle animals? This can't be right."
>
> The abbot addressed the community. "Look, there are hunters in these mountains. The only defence these animals have is their fear. If you take that away from them, they will all be killed very soon."
>
> If we were fearless, we like the deer, would be in terrible danger and not know it. When one is frightened, one is acutely aware of their surroundings. It motivates us and gets us moving. Fear also galvanizes. It promotes feats of strength and mental acuity; all our resources are mobilized. Most of us have

> heard about the grandmother who with super-human strength, lifts the car off her son when it falls on him when he is underneath fixing the muffler. Little or no fear tends to make us lazy, bored, or complacent. We need fear to live and stay alive.

Closely related to fear is love. We lose sensitivity for those around us by suppressing the awareness of our own vulnerability. Admitting vulnerability to a comrade helps develop the intimate relation needed to survive and support each other during combat operations. (Keep your head on swivel.) The fear one feels for others is the most wrenching experience of all. One fears for the other when one loves. One watches out for them, when one fears for them, just as a mother is fearful for her child, like a mother duck looking after her brood. The mother duck will die protecting her ducklings. In this sense, leaders are like mothers looking after their troops. Look after your soldiers and they will look after you is a common refrain. And, troops look after one another instinctively, (guard my six, cover me I'm going in) is common soldier lingo. A collective despair, fueled by fear, or what I call shared suffering, bonds soldiers together in a common, communal effort. Soldiers are often quoted as saying "I fought for my buddies on my left and right."[10]

Fear can stay with you long after the incident that caused it. Often fear doesn't leave, and it becomes what author Daisy Hernandez calls "a second skin."[11] This is perhaps where the term 'thick skin' comes from.

Noble silence has been taught in some circles of meditation, but author Audre Lorde, a Black feminist poet, in a speech in 1977 before she died, contradicts this and warns us against the "tyrannies of silence." She declared that we should speak out about our fears, saying "your silence will not protect you." Tibetan Buddhism offers methods and techniques to recognize and overcome fear. Applying breathing techniques our mental energy becomes clearer, and we begin to feel revitalized and able to overcome anxiety. Many individuals with anxiety are often frightened by the physical feelings triggered by dangerous situations such as a rapidly beating heart, hyperventilation, tight chest muscles, contracted abdominal muscles and a dizzy feeling along with foreboding of catastrophic events.

The esteemed Harvard Psychologist, Daniel Wegner has noted that "when we stop suppressing our emotional experience, stress and anxiety are invariably alleviated."[12] To alleviate fear, we as leaders can build teamwork and cohesion; keep our people informed of the mission, the changing situation, and overall picture; and lead by example.

3.2.4 Anxiety

Operational stress injuries, also called combat stress injuries (CSIs), include several inter connected and co-morbid ailments and disorders. Among these is the second most prevalent disorder in the CF behind depression: anxiety. According to M. Shields in her *Social Anxiety Disorder*, anxiety can be caused by myriad triggers:

Anxiety can occur in a variety of circumstances from everyday problems (stress at work or home) to feeling that a person's life is in danger. Some life situations that could cause anxiety are postings, deployment, family separation (due to training or Imposed Restriction) divorce, illness or death of a friend or family member, loss of health or accidents. The situation does not have to be negative to cause anxiety. Events like marriage, promotion, retirement, a birth or graduation can create a high level of anxiety in a person also.[13]

A few of these signs do not by themselves prove that a soldier is experiencing anxiety, nevertheless, they are warning signs and must be taken seriously and evaluated by professional clinicians.

People with anxiety disorders show excessive levels of apprehension and angst that significantly interfere with daily life. Normal anxiety is limited in severity and time. Anxiety disorders are different from normal anxiety in that: They are more severe and intense, long lasting, interfering with a person's ability to function and occurring even when danger is not imminent.[14] A 'fight or flight' or freeze' response is the normal reaction to excessive anxiety. An anxiety disorder affects how a person thinks, behaves and feels. If not treated, it could develop into a chronic condition and cause serious disability like Major Depression (MD), PTSD, substance abuse and other comorbidities. For Regular Force veterans who released from the service in 1998-2011, anxiety disorders were tied in with PTSD for second place after mood disorders in prevalence.[15]

Anxiety disorders can be triggered by traumatic events. More than 70% of people with anxiety disorder have one or more other diagnosable mental health problems like depressive mood disorder, misuse of substances or personality disorder.[16] A high level of anxiety over a long period of time will often lead to depression. Many people have a mixture of anxiety and depression as a result.[17] Anxiety can manifest itself in a variety of ways, both psychological and physical.

Psychological effects include fear, trepidation, sense of impending doom or imminent danger causing inappropriate and excessive worry. The environment feels unreal and unfamiliar, producing a feeling of detachment and distraction. Decreased attention and concentration cause a speeding and slowing of thoughts. A fear of dying or going mad causes irritability, insomnia and vivid dreams.

Physical symptoms include cardiovascular effects such as heart palpitations, chest pain, rapid heart rate, and flushing along with respiratory (hyperventilation, shortness of breath). Neurological consequences include dizziness, headache, vertigo, and tingling or numbness of the skin. Gastrointestinal outcomes are choking, dry mouth, nausea, vomiting, and diarrhea. Musculoskeletal outcomes are muscle ache and tension, and restlessness.[18]

People who demonstrate five of these symptoms have a 50% chance of being afflicted with a mental health problem. With more symptoms, the probability rises sharply.[19]

The main anxiety disorders include generalized anxiety disorder, (GAD), panic attack and agoraphobia._The main symptom of GAD is overwhelming anxiety and worry experienced more days than not for at least six months. GAD can make it almost impossible to concentrate at work, function at home, and enjoy normal living.[20]A panic attack is when intense fear inappropriate to the situation in which it is occurring; symptoms reach their peak abruptly in about ten minutes. They are similar to a heart attack and the victim has a feeling of dying or impending doom.[21]_Agoraphobia is the intense fear of having a panic attack or symptoms and becoming embarrassed or humiliated in a place where help or escape may not be available. Sufferers might avoid being outside their house alone, using public transportation or standing in lines.[22] Other anxiety disorders include special phobia disorders which restrict activities in specific locations or situations due to excessive or irrational fear, which is persistent and causes unreasonable impairment and undue stress. (i.e. seeing blood, travelling on buses, planes and trains or over bridges and high-level roads.[23]

3.2.5. Post-Traumatic Stress Disorder (PTSD) and Acute Stress Disorder

Trauma-related disorders include acute stress disorder (ASD) and post-traumatic stress disorder (PTSD). PTSD is of great concern in armies of the western alliance. Anxiety and depression are the other main disorders that plague Canadian warriors with combat experience, but PTSD is most often blamed for both suicides and criminal acts. PTSD, although not the most prevalent mental health disorder, appears to be the most harmful and troubling illness for CF soldiers and is blamed for the most incidents of suicide or attempted suicide. ASD is similar and related to PTSD.[24]

Many of the symptoms of ASD and PTSD are the same, but the criteria for diagnosis are different. The symptoms will normally dissipate within a month with acute stress disorder. Some individuals with ASD will develop PTSD if the criteria continue to be met, and if their response to the traumatic event caused intense fear, horror or helplessness and vulnerability. PTSD occurs after experiencing a severely distressing or catastrophic event which involves near-death or threat of serious injury or witnessing such an occurrence.[25]

Traumatic incidents may be such incidents as an encounter improvised explosive devices, witnessing violence or the aftermath of violence, (especially when rules of engagement do not allow intervention), sexual assault, torture, being kidnapped or held captive, child abuse, vehicle accidents, train wrecks, plane crashes, bombings, natural disasters or being ordered or forced to inflict violence on others. PTSD sufferers have a six times higher risk of attempting suicide than those who have no mental health problem. With early diagnoses, and treatment however, many do recover or manage their illness.[26]

Symptoms of PTSD and ASD include the re-experiencing of the trauma (i.e. recurrent dreams of the event, flashbacks, and intrusive memories along with feelings of uneasiness that bring back memories of the event, which in turn produces avoidance behaviour of associated things. The effect is an emotional numbing with reduced interest in the outside world that may continue for months, and even years. More troubling signs are increased sensory arousal, with constant watchfulness, irritability, jumpiness, increased startle response, outbursts of rage, and periods of insomnia. All ranks must be familiar with these tell-tale symptoms in themselves, their peers, their subordinates, and their superiors. All ranks must also know what to do about it.

3.2.6. Addiction

Addiction is a common result of OSIs. Soldiers suffering from any of the stress injuries regardless of the cause turn to self-medication with alcohol or drugs. Alcohol is a depressant, and can act quickly to relive feelings of anxiety, but long-term alcohol abuse and subsequent withdrawal can increase anxiety levels. This can become a vicious circle where this makes day-to-day living at home and work more difficult which in turn creates continued and often increased stress. The same thing can happen with other drugs such as stimulants, opiates, cannabis, and even caffeine. People might start out using these substances to treat pain, create alertness, or calm nerves, but self-medicating never works in the long term. Many substances have side effects that will make the underlying conditions of depression and anxiety worse, potentially triggering psychosis and other severe responses.

The CF provides several services for addictions of all types, including gambling and drugs. These are health promotion; assessment and referral; secondary substance intervention; outpatient counseling; and residential treatment programs, after care, and follow-up. All of these programs have proven effective and have save countless careers and lives.

3.2.6. Suicide

According to Antoon Leenaars, an expert on suicide prevention, based in Windsor Ontario, suicide is epidemic in the Canadian military. Over the past fifteen years, there were 103 deaths by suicide among Regular Force males in the Army. All other branches account for seventy-two. Between 2010 and 2014, the Army had forty suicides compared to twelve non-Army members.

The Army suicide rate per 100,000 people is four times the civilian rate and three times the rate for other branches of the CF and this does not include veterans or female soldiers.

It goes without saying that currently suicide is a very concerning problem in the CF. Studies have shown that those who serve in the Army are four times more likely to kill themselves than the general population. Previous studies have also shown that veterans are more at risk than active members[27]. As recently as 11 November 2017, The CF Chaplain General, Brigadier-General Guy Chapdelaine, clad in the white robes of his office, delivered a powerful message to those struggling with thoughts of suicide as a result of their time in uniform. He prayed for those who died defending Canada before turning to "soldiers suffering from injuries visible and invisible."[28] It was a poignant moment and resonated with all in attendance at the War Memorial in Ottawa commemorating Remembrance Day.

4.0. A Leader's Response to OSIs

Understanding the severity of these issues, what can leaders do?_An increased risk of suicidal behaviour is associated with anxiety disorders, especially if depression is also present. In comparison to the general public, the CF rates are ten or more times higher.[29] Effective and proactive leadership is key to preventing and mitigating OSIs. Troop morale and mental health can be maintained and even improved by close and careful adherence to the Principles of Leadership and the Principles of War and other leadership strategies. Trust and loyalty can be kept at a high level when the troops know that leaders are competent and have the knowledge and training to produce the best possible plans and preparations to ensure success in battle. Just as leaders and fellow soldiers must provide physical first aid, when mental health crisis does occur, the first reaction of the leader must be to apply Crisis First Aid.

4.1. Crisis First Aid

Mental Health First Aid measures first call for one to listen non-judgmentally while assessing the risk of suicide or causing harm to self or others. At the same time, one should give reassurance and information to get the appropriate professional help. As leaders, we should let the person tell the story at their own pace in their own words. It may also be good to offer practical help for the necessities of life if needed, including accommodation, food, and contact with family. It is imperative upon every leader in the Canadian Forces to be aware of what resources the CF has available to provide assistance.[30]

5.0 Military Leadership

General Rick Hillier, the CDS during much of the Afghanistan War, wrote some profound things in his visceral foreword to *Leadership in the Canadian Forces*:

> For the Canadian Forces to continue to be relevant, responsive and effective in today's complex, and often dangerous battlespace, requires outstanding leaders at all ranks and all levels—tactical, operational and strategic. Leaders with an operational focus. Leaders capable of executing and empowered to execute, a mission command philosophy in accordance with the CF values-based leadership doctrine.... CF military professionals can build and shape their leader skills and techniques to direct, enable and motivate their followers in the successful achievement of a wide range of assigned tasks from day-to-day garrison duty to domestic operations up the scale to humanitarian aid, peace keeping to peace making and combat.[31]

Overall the CF is effective when it is accomplishing missions endorsed by Canadians at large. This includes engaging fellow citizens; and adapting to external change in society and government. Effectiveness is also based on showing honest and genuine concern for all members of the CF while building teams that are synchronized in support of the larger organization. All of this must be accomplished in concert with values and norms that are embraced by Canadians.

This gives the CF a reputation for effectiveness and legitimacy in the eyes of the public. This should give the CF and its leaders the full trust, confidence and above all support and funding of the Government of Canada.

Effective leadership in the Canadian Forces is defined in *Leadership in the Canadian Forces: Doctrine*, as "directing, motivating and enabling others to accomplish the mission professionally and ethically, while developing or improving capabilities that contribute to mission success."[32] For this essay, I will use the Infantry Battalion as a model to illustrate techniques, procedures and principles of leadership designed to maintain high morale

Leaders must "achieve professional competence" is the first Principle of Leadership in CFP (Canadian Forces Pamphlet) 131(1) para 405. Major General Dan Spry, RCR, a Division Commander during the War, told me that in the '30s, when he was a subaltern, that he and his fellow officers spent at least one hour per day studying and debating combat techniques. This went on for years and put them in good stead to go to war.[33] Their studies included proficiency with weapons, tactics, planning, physical training and administration and logistics. We learn from history. We hone our skills with education, training practice and the inevitable mistakes which all teach us something important. The best leaders learn from the successes, failures and mistakes of others. Modern soldiers deserve as much from their leaders. To gain the trust of their men, leaders must know their job.

5.1.1. Infantry Training and Leadership

Sections and platoons are the teams upon which the success of the battalion rests. The battalion is the first self-sustaining unit in the order of battle. Probably the most difficult leadership challenge in the Army is commanding an Infantry unit. Infantry are invariably the largest contingent on the battlefield and suffer the most casualties because of their proximity to the enemy, their vulnerability and their mission to 'close with and destroy the enemy' and hold ground after it has been captured.[34]

Infantry leaders also, invariably, have the largest number of subordinates in their sphere of influence. A section commander, platoon commander, company commander or even battalion commander, who are face to face and constantly observed by their troops, should keep calm and decisive to maintain the confidence of their troops.

A leader must first have the confidence and trust of their troops, and to gain this they must have confidence in themselves. To have justified this confidence they must know their job by rote. They must be able to make up their mind and make up their mind quickly to formulate a plan and see it through to fruition. A determined, stout-hearted leader will instill their own fighting spirit into their followers.

Another essential of leadership is loyalty. A leader must be loyal to their peers and their superiors if they expect loyalty from their subordinates. Finally, and no less important the leader must understand and practice discipline and self-discipline. Above all, they must be firm but fair and always employ common sense. Success or failure in battle will depend largely on the effective tactical handling of sub-units and the initiative of junior leaders.

5.1.2. Discipline and Administration in the Field

Discipline in the field is closely connected with the care of the troops. The care of their soldiers is the first responsibility of all commanders. Leaders must constantly look after the welfare and interests of their soldiers. Leaders must 'know' their men and women, particularly their capabilities and characteristics. A sense of comradeship, and bonding should be encouraged between officers, Non-Commissioned Officers, (NCOs) and other ranks. To be fair, leaders at all levels must ensure that extra duties and fatigues are divided equally. Mail should be distributed and posted as soon as possible. Any sickness or injury must be tended to immediately. Care and comforts of soldiers must be a priority, during quiet/rest periods as well as in action. Boredom can be troublesome and distracting.

5.1.2.1. Roll Books

Roll books should be kept by all leaders to include such details as number, rank, languages, religion, and medical information.[35] This information will frequently become very important.

Leaders are responsible for the fitness and health of their soldiers; they must be constantly monitoring signs of strain, exhaustion or illness. High standards of sanitation and hygiene are imperative. Questionable water sources should always be sterilized with tablets or by boiling. As we avoid and recover physical casualties, we must also avert and heal OSIs.

We have probably all been involved in casualty evacuation of a comrade on exercise or in operations. Care is immediate and obvious. Fewer of us have been involved with a mental health casualty. This is not so immediate and not so obvious. To be effective we must know as much about mental health as we know about physical health and how to apply mental health first aid. To sum it up: "the good officer or NCO knows his men well and is always in evidence after a really arduous, tiring day. While the indifferent leader will probably be busy seeing to his own comfort. The good leader will be looking after the care and comfort of his soldiers."[36]

5.1.2.1. Discipline

It is imperative that an Army have good discipline to promote efficiency and effectiveness. Discipline is based on duty, self-respect and self-control; it is a state of mind where an individual does his duty regardless of being under supervision or not. It is what one does when nobody is watching.

5.1.2.3. Administration in the Field

Essential to the maintenance of morale is sound administration, especially in the field and on deployment where supports and comforts are often limited. As mentioned above, it is the first duty of the section, platoon, and company commanders to see to the needs and comfort of their men. It is important for all leaders to be in-sync to avoid duplication, double tasking, and contradictory orders.

5.1.2.4. Routine

Routine is important in both garrison and the field and is doubly important in operations. Routine helps to ensure that no points of administration are overlooked; ensures that high standards are maintained; and avoids any unfairness in distribution of duties and fatigues. Less vital, but still important, it also relieves boredom during quiet periods out of action.

Daily inspections of weapons and ammunition must be carried out. Other equipment should be inspected, maintained and replaced if necessary. Complaints concerning quantity and quality of rations should be investigated and rectified if necessary. Smoke, fire, movement, light and noise discipline should be observed day and night when in close contact with the enemy. Included in routine should be times for meals, washing and shaving, sick parade, and church parade. Inspections should encompass arms and ammunition, and equipment, tools and uniforms. Feet should be inspected regularly, especially after long marches and inclement weather. Rest periods should be scheduled daily. Forced rest may be required to prepare for a long and arduous tasking.

5.1.2.5. Training

Traditionally, armies from ancient times have reorganized continually in an effort to improve their capability and success in battle. Often, this only aggravated professional soldiers as indicated by Petronius Arbiter, a leader in the Roman Army who wrote in 210 BC:

We trained hard...but it seemed every time we were beginning to form up into teams we would be reorganized... I was to learn later in life that we tend to meet any new situation by reorganizing; and a wonderful method it can be in creating the illusion of progress while producing confusion, inefficiency and demoralization.[37] We must avoid this constant reorganizing at all costs.

Training must be regular, progressive and carefully planned to be realistic, tough and demanding. This is vital to maintaining confidence and efficiency in war fighting. Leaders must be proficient in weapons, battle craft and battle procedure. Battlecraft is standard operational procedures (SOPs) or drills to tackling minor tactical problems where rapid reaction and movement is needed for success. Battlecraft includes such techniques as formations for the advance to contact and the attack, fire and movement, patrolling, fire control, field signals, camouflage and concealment, layout of defensive positions and construction of fire trenches and bunkers. Resupply procedures should also be practiced (without combat supplies, soldiers can't fight). And probably most important for morale, battlefield first aid, handling of casualties and casualty evacuation must be rehearsed.

5.1.2.6. Battle Procedure

Battle procedure includes such complimentary and progressive methods as time appreciation, warning order, reconnaissance, battle appreciation, and orders. This ensures concurrent activity in preparation for battle which keeps all ranks active in contributing to the success of the operation. Knowing that plans and preparation are completed in meticulous detail gives the troops and leaders a sense of community, confidence and trust which promotes mental wellness. Familiar formats also help with rapid understanding of the overall plan and Commander's intent. And if the unit can strike faster than the enemy, the chance of winning is significantly enhanced. Like a gunfight— draw faster and shoot straighter—you win and stay alive.

5.1.2.6.1. The Time Appreciation

The time appreciation should allow subordinates enough time to do their reconnaissance, planning and orders. It works out the time available between the receipt of the original orders and the start, or H hour, of the mission. Factors to be considered should be time/space i.e. how long does it take to get from the current location to the jumping-off point or Start Line (SL) of the operation in the attack. In the defence, how long does it take to get from current location to the defensive or blocking position? How long does it take to prepare the defensive position?

In the other major operation, the withdrawal, timings are critical to make a clean break from the enemy. The stages of the withdrawal include the movement of the reconnaissance party to set up the new position, the time for thinning out, move of the main body and finally the move back of the covering party. Other major operations are the advance and encounter battle, the raid and the ambush; all requiring careful planning in time/space. Patrols, both standing and active are also a complicated operation and require detailed consideration of timings and distances to be covered.

5.1.2.6.2. Warning Order

The warning order should be issued as soon as instructions/orders are received for the operation. The warning order should at the least include: A rough outline and forecast of operations; and a rendezvous for the Orders (O) group. Any special administrative instructions to prepare for battle i.e. special weapons and equipment to be carried and when and where individual or sub-units grouped together will meet up. And finally, most important to all concerned, the expected time to move out, "No move before ... hours or "be at ... hours notice to move."

In sum, the warning order allows all commanders time to do their planning simultaneously while the troops complete administrative preparations (concurrent activity) for the operation (i.e. prepare weapons and equipment; rehearsals if necessary, food and rest).

5.1.2.6.3. Reconnaissance

Reconnaissance (recce) is a vital step in the operational planning sequence. In it the leader will first procure any intelligence concerning the mission, study the map or any air photos available to glean as much information as possible about the ground and enemy dispositions if available as well as likely viewpoints, routes and obstacles, distances etc. They will then make a reconnaissance plan. The commander must consider time available to ensure that they have sufficient time to complete their appreciation/estimate, plan, and orders. Also, they must concern themselves with giving each of their subordinates time to complete their recce and orders.

5.1.2.6.4. Planning

We have already discussed time appreciation, battle procedure, and warning order. The next step in the sequence is the battle appreciation, commonly referred to as the 'appreciation' or 'combat estimate.' Basically, it amounts to thinking out the problem in a logical sequence to arrive at a workable plan. The minimum format is as follows. The aim to be achieved; and the factors which affect the attainment of this aim. The most important are the ground and the relative strength of the enemy and own troops. The calculation of time and space, that is the time it takes to cover distance by both vehicle and on foot, are important to successfully completing any mission or phases of an operation. Every factor considered must be followed by a deduction. Factors with no useful deduction(s) should be discarded immediately to avoid confusion. Finally, out of this comes courses open to one's own troops and enemy; and this all leads to the plan.

5.1.2.6.5. Orders

Generally, orders are given, mostly verbally, at the platoon, company and battalion level. At section level they are always given verbally due to time restraints. After orders are given, all concerned should know what their commander intends to do, how he intends to do it, and what part they will play in the operation. Orders are given in a logical sequence outlined below to ensure that nothing important is forgotten. Being used to this format the recipients can quickly and easily grasp the details of their task and the tasks of their sister sub-units. As long as nothing critical is omitted, the shorter the orders the better to allow subordinates to complete their battle procedure and planning.

Orders should be given if possible where the recipients can see the ground. If this is not possible, a map, air photograph, or model can be used. The commander must first point out on the ground or map, or model, the features and points on the ground that they will refer to and then give their orders in the following format, with which all ranks are familiar.

- *Situation.* The current situation regarding the enemy and own troops, including enemy dispositions, strength and morale will be discussed. Own troops will cover details of flanking sub-units and units and supporting arms, and service support elements.
- *Attachments and Detachments.* This will cover any support arms in direct support; and any detachments to be sent to other units/sub-units.
- *Mission.* The mission will clearly state the intention of the commander and what each component will do (but not how) this is up to the commander at each level.
- *Execution.* The execution paragraph_will describe briefly and clearly how the commander intends to carry out the mission. Who does what.
- *Co-ordinating Instructions*. Coordinating instructions are a number of measures that ensure coordination and cooperation of all units and sub units involved. Examples are timings, report lines, routes, axis of advance, assembly areas, boundaries and signals.
- *Administration and Logistics.* Here, the commander directs any changes to the normal resupply and administrative procedures. Also, the issue of any special weapons or equipment will be outlined along with ammunition resupply, medical and feeding arrangements, and rest. timings.
- *Command and Signals.* The location of Headquarters, the commanding officer, along with nicknames, code words, report lines, alternate commanders, and other information will be included.
- *Frequencies.* Radio frequencies will be allocated as necessary and confirmed.

- *Signals.* Details of any pre-arranged signals will be given along with passwords and nicknames, including smoke, light, audio signal, tracer fire, and others.

5.1.2.7. Resiliency

As leaders we are responsible for developing resiliency in both ourselves and our followers. To do this, leaders must be alert to the occurrence of crisis events; and ever vigilant in recognizing the effects and symptoms of crisis, fear and stress not only on subordinates, but also on themselves and their superiors.

It doesn't matter why someone is exhibiting warning signs and symptoms of MH problems. A leader's role, regardless, is to support them and help them to recover. To simplify this process, it is divided into three distinct stages or zones: Yellow = Reacting; Green = Ready; and Orange = Injured. Proper handling of people in the Yellow/Reacting zone is critical. The AIM is to get them back to the Green/Ready zone.

Improper handling resulting from a lack of awareness on the part of the leader, or withdrawal of support by peers, could well push someone into the Orange/Injured zone. Leaders and Peers are in a position to help ensure that they bounce back to Green and do not slip into the Orange zone. Self-care is also critical for a leader to stay healthy and effective. If you're drowning in a bucket of crisis induced stress, and heading into the Yellow/Reacting zone, you can't be the kind of leader your subordinates are counting on. Self-care strategies should be seriously and regularly observed.

6.1. Critical Requirements of an Effective Leader

According to *Leadership in the Canadian Forces* LEADING PEOPLE, 2007, there are ten critical requirements of an effective leader: A successful leader seeks and accepts responsibility and accountability; performs effectively under stress; skillfully applies skills and knowledge; demonstrates initiative and decisiveness; seeks and accepts advice and constructive criticism; and inspires team spirit, performance and co-operation. Most importantly, a successful leader plans effectively, communicates effectively, supervises effectively, and delegates effectively.

To be able to plan effectively, a leader must know tactics and battle procedure by rote. They must know how to decipher and use maps, sketches and air and satellite photos and navigate by compass and the sun and stars, since GPS might be knocked out. To read the ground is an innate talent, but it can be learned with practice and study. Knowing weapons ranges and characteristics is essential to ensure optimum deployment of all arms.

An effective leader communicates effectively. Accurate and effective communication between all ranks, particularly commanders and subordinates, is key to success. Familiar formats for orders and instructions, normally found in standard operating procedures (SOPs), should be used for all operations. Important information should be read back at orders groups to ensure understanding, particularly timings, code words, and passwords. Written orders should be clear and concise, using simple language and acronyms understood by all ranks.

Effective supervisors will visit their subordinates to talk face-to-face before an operation begins, or while it is under way, if possible. It is important to ensure that units and sub-units are in the right place at the right time and oriented as required. Also, necessary adjustments can be made as indicated and any further or clarifying instructions can be given. Checking to confirm that weapons and equipment are in-situ is another supervisors duty.

A good leader delegates effectively. Leaders must delegate tasks that have to be completed concurrently. Alternate commanders must be appointed should commanders become casualties to re-establish the chain of command. The commander's intent must be clearly established to allow all subordinate commanders to carry on despite death and destruction.

6.2. Principles of Leadership

Principles of Leadership are time-tested tenets and axioms to guide leaders, both young and old, in all ranks, on how to command their troops in the most efficient and effective manner. Leaders are given the honour and privilege to control the efforts of their soldiers while moving in to harm's way. To be ready they would profit much from careful study and application of these principles listed below.

There are thirteen principles now. Half a dozen iterations have been published during the last fifty years with at least ten principles saying the same thing, but in different words. These requirements are closely related and complimentary to the Requirements of an Effective Leader, above, which provide guidance and organize succinctly both the theory and the practice of effective leadership. The principles of leadership are:

- Achieve professional competence and seek self-improvement;
- Clarify objectives and intent;
- Solve problems and make timely decisions;
- Direct; motivate by persuasion and example and by sharing risks and hardships (that is, lead by example);
- Train under demanding and realistic conditions;
- Build teamwork and cohesion;
- Keep subordinates informed;
- Mentor, educate and develop subordinates;
- Treat subordinates fairly;
- Maintain situational awareness, seek information and keep current
- Learn from experience and those who have experience;
- Exemplify and reinforce the military ethos;
- maintain good order and discipline; and
- uphold professional norms (that is, lead by example).

6.3. Morale

High morale is pearl of very great value, and most important in war. Numbers, armaments and resources cannot compensate for the lack of courage, energy, determination, skill and bold offensive spirit. Field Marshall Viscount Bernard Montgomery, of Alamein, the WW2 British Army Group Commander, who defeated Rommel, the famous German Desert Fox, in the harsh and boundless North African landscape, summed it up best when he wrote in his advice to all commanders:

"[s]study the factor of morale; it is the big thing in war and without high morale, you can achieve nothing." Inspiration and guidance must come from the commander, and it must permeate throughout the force. Without good morale, success in battle is very illusive.

All operations in war must have a good and reasonable chance of success. High morale is based on discipline, self-respect and the trust and confidence of the soldier in his commanders, support units, and weapons and equipment and perhaps most important, his peers. Maintenance of Morale has been proven in historical studies as second only to Maintenance of the Aim in the hierarchy of The Principles of War. If morale is good, the chance of success is good.

Morale is affected both positively and negatively by several related and complimentary factors. Trusting their superiors to provide the weapons, organization and a winning tactical plan along with the administrative and logistics support to ensure success is foremost in the minds of all soldiers. Commanders at all levels are chosen for their qualities of leadership: they have initiative, drive and an ability to inspire confidence in their subordinates. All ranks must be convinced that they are trusted and valued by superiors, subordinates and most important peers and comrades. Trust and respect up and down the chain of command is vital for good morale.

At Vimy, as discussed in *Volume 2 of Canadians and War*, "Vimy Ridge," all arms available in the Corps, and any others that could be bargained for, cajoled from Allies or stolen (from whoever) were made available. The innovative organization of the units and sub units in teams that could fight together employing fire and movement techniques and leap frog bounds, not to mention the brilliant counter battery methods, was innovative and overwhelmed the enemy quickly. But, the main factor was the men's determination, loyalty and devotion to each other created by high morale. A Vietnam veteran, who served in the Infantry, when questioned about what he worried about in combat replied, "I look after anything to my immediate front and my buddies to my left and right."

To the astonishment of many, especially the Allied generals, the tactical plan for Vimy was ingenious, innovative, all inclusive, and ultimately successful. General, later Sir Arthur Currie, and staff had meticulously, thoughtfully, and thoroughly planned the attack. The troops knew that (mainly because they trained constantly, with almost daily rehearsals, and were briefed in what some called nauseating detail) but they were found comfort by the power of it all. There was a beehive of activity in the Corps area with preparations for administration and logistics, concentrating on casualty evacuation, resupply, reinforcements and several complimentary communications systems. As well, the junior leaders at the lowest level were allowed to use their initiative (British and French troops were not) for the first time for many, to act independently against targets or situations of opportunity and coordinate with flanking and depth reinforcement teams, for mutual support. All designated junior leaders were issued with maps as well, for the first time, to assist with navigation and coordination. More pedestrian, but equally as important, to all ranks, mail continued to be delivered and dispatched, up until the last minute. And finally, the rum issue was given often and in quantity which never failed to lift the spirits of the men. The Ridge was within their grasp. Morale was high.

6.4. Military Ethos and Values

Mission success is values based. That is, it must be done professionally and ethically in accordance with the CF military ethos. The military ethos consists of three components: beliefs and expectations about military service, fundamental Canadian values, and core military values.

6.4.1. Beliefs and Expectations

The soldier's beliefs and expectations about military service must be defined and promoted. These include explaining the concepts of unlimited liability, the fighting spirit, teamwork and discipline and self discipline. Each of these separately and in concert are most important to victory on the battlefield. They must be closely observed and monitored by leaders.

6.4.1.1. Unlimited Liability

Unlimited liability means accepting the fact that soldiers can be lawfully ordered into harm's way in conditions that could lead to injury or loss of life. This is one rule of law that separates soldiers from civilians. In short, they are to salute smartly and get on with the job, regardless of the perils involved. Soldiers have sworn to serve Canada before self; this exemplifies the first core military value of duty. The Royal Military College (RMC) motto is "Truth, Duty, Valour."

6.4.1.2. Fighting Spirit

For leaders to be effective in battle, they must have what we call fighting spirit. Leaders who embrace the fighting spirit are not intimidated by danger or adversity. They develop a competitive spirit in their followers seeking to prevail in all tasks and missions. It gives soldiers the intellectual, moral and physical traits required for them to endure hardship, extreme danger and approach their assignments with tenacity and confidence. They have the will to win.

6.4.1.3. Discipline and Self-Discipline

Discipline and self-discipline are key to success in war. Discipline instills shared values and common standards, allowing compliance with the goals and interests of the unit or sub-unit. Leaders should always encourage self-discipline which supports initiative, innovation and independent action.

6.4.1.4. Teamwork

The army is a collective endeavour and relies on teamwork throughout the chain of command. teamwork, by its nature, uses the talent and skills of the group to leverage the success of operations and prevail in battle. Teamwork also creates a sense of belonging which in turn precipitates high morale. Joining the army means that each soldier is part of a force much bigger than self. The terms army and teamwork are synonymous.

6.4.2. Fundamental Canadian Values

The Statement of Defence Ethics requires soldiers to respect the dignity of all persons and support and obey lawful authority that is both international and national law. No one is above the 'rule of law. '*The National Defence Act, Queen's Regulations and Orders* outline the lawful authority of superiors and the Code of Service Discipline provides coercive element to this lawful authority.

Internationally, *Jus ad bellum* (the law toward war) governs and seeks to limit resorting to armed force among belligerents, it seeks to moderate the actual conduct of hostilities. Its main sources are the *Geneva Conventions* of 1949 and *The Hague Conventions* of 1899 and 1907. Victims of armed conflict are protected by the Geneva articles and The Hague law is concerned with methods and means of warfare. These conventions regulate military necessity, due proportionality, and humanity. Rules of Engagement (ROEs), which will be discussed later in further detail, are guided by both national and international law.

Civic values in Canada are expressed in the Canadian Charter of Rights and Freedoms (1982) supporting equal rights regardless of race, colour, religion, language, gender, sexual orientation, or ethnic origin.

6.4.3. Core Military Values

Core military values are duty, loyalty, integrity, and courage. They are instilled in soldiers by training and practical and authentic field exercises. These values are designed to inculcate a sense of belonging, trust, and an innate understanding of right and wrong. Canadian core values separate our soldiers from those of many other nations.

6.4.3.1. Duty

Duty obliges soldiers to show dedication, initiative and discipline. Leaders are obliged to serve Canada before self to achieve mission success while simultaneously ensuring the well-being of their subordinates. The motto of the American Heroes Chanel (AHC) on television, which showcases military triumphs and failures, is "Duty

Honour Courage." This parallels the Canadian concept of values. All ranks would profit from watching it.

6.4.3.2. Loyalty

Loyalty entails faithfulness to comrades, and allegiance to Canada and the rule of law. Loyalty involves mutual trust. Loyalty is not just up but down and sideways in the chain of command. Leaders must be loyal to both their superiors and their subordinates along with their peers. This, in time, will encourage loyalty throughout the army.

6.4.3.4. Integrity

Leaders must be accountable for their actions and fully committed to moral obligations and moral conduct. At all times, they must exhibit uprightness, truthfulness, honesty and adherence to the highest ethical standards. Leaders are constantly under the scrutiny of their soldiers as well as their bosses; they don't get away with much if anything. Lead by example, and make sure your example is good.

6.4.3.5. Courage

Leaders must embrace both moral and physical courage. This allows a leader to carry on despite physical difficulty, risk or popularity of decisions, and entails both resolve and willpower. Leaders make values real by consistently living by them, demonstrating and instilling the military ethos in others and facing and resolving problems ethically, fairly, and lawfully. Courage is not fearlessness, but a determination to carry on despite fear in both action and daily life.

6.4.3.6. Distributive Leadership

Combat effectiveness depends on developing a strong officer/NCM team with shared responsibility, professional identity, values and purpose and mutually supporting expertise. Distributive leadership, commonly known as delegation of authority, is about sharing responsibilities of leadership vertically and horizontally with teams and groups at all levels of command. The leadership potential of all leaders down to the lowest level of designated authority should be leveraged, developed and exploited.

6.4.3.7. Followership

All leaders in the CF are also followers. Even the CDS has a boss, the MND, Minister of National Defence. Critical to effective leadership is understanding effective followership. Effective followers are valued, and essential members of the team committed to serve the CF. They get the job done regardless of supervision and are receptive to and implementers of innovation and change. Without followers, you don't need leaders.[38]

7.0. Leadership and Mitigating OSIs

What, exactly do leaders have to deal with in their attempt to mitigate OSIs? What should we know? It is imperative that we know how to maintain physical fitness in both garrison and during field exercises and deployments; what fitness and lifestyle evaluation programs are available and considerations for nutrition, sleep, and safety; signs of stigma, and the leader's responsibility to deal with stigma.

7.1. Leader's Wellness

Physical fitness, nutrition, sleep, and safety are the main wellness factors. Good physical fitness is an obvious and commonly accepted method of reducing stress and being battle ready. Also, it goes without saying that nutrition is a major requirement for physical and mental fitness. And, of course, everyone knows that a lack of sleep can reduce physical performance and mental acuity significantly. Safety is maintained by a combination of these factors along with providing adequate shelter when required. As leaders we must lead by example by maintaining our own personal fitness and wellbeing and ensuring that we look after our troops as well as possible.

7.1.1. Physical Fitness

Physical fitness is paramount to overall wellness. "A sound mind in a sound body" as Socrates wrote over two millennia ago. Physical fitness is one of the trademarks of CF soldiers, combat arms, Infantry. Leaders are responsible to ensure that all troops under their command are encouraged to maintain battle fitness which includes physical as well as mental wellness. This is another opportunity to set and live the example.

Most physical fitness work is done in garrison, but it can also be conducted during field training and even on operations. Chief Warrant Officer T. J. Secretan, after his deployment to Operation Kinetic in Kosovo, speaks of the work done to maintain troop health and fitness there:

We in the Air Force pay lip service to fitness. We continually find excuses to avoid implementing a unit fitness plan. During my deployment to Kosovo was evident that those members of the unit who has a fitness program back in Canada were better equipped to endure the long hours and 40+ C heat. I have been a long-time believer in physical fitness, and even though it may seem like a waste of sea container space, we did bring a small amount of fitness equipment with us. Once we had settled into a steady routine, everyone in camp was encouraged to maintain or improve his or her fitness. The gym was in use 24/7.[39]

7.1.2. Available Resources

A strategy was launched by the CDS on 31 March 2008. The vision was to provide ways and means for every CF member to attain their personal health and physical fitness sufficient to meet operational requirements. The military has a long tradition of promoting and measuring physical fitness. The new strategy recognizes that mental health is equally important to operational readiness. Health is defined broadly and encompasses physical, mental and social fitness. It's more than the absence of disease. It's a lifestyle, not a task. The strategy stresses that the C of C at all levels will be held responsible for ensuring widespread support of healthy lifestyle behaviour. They will be expected to lead by example and to provide the time, resources, and programs for CF personnel to participate.

The Health and Physical Fitness Strategy identifies the importance of an addiction-free lifestyle and healthy coping. Military members cope with situations and stressors other Canadians do not. The CF provides many support services to assist members and their leaders. *Strengthening the Forces Health Promotion* professionals on all Bases/Wings offer a myriad of courses and services related to healthy coping and mental and social fitness. They include Stress: Take Charge, Managing Angry Moments, Applied Suicide Intervention Skills Training, Basic Relationship Training: Stronger Together Relationship Skills for CF Couples, Alcohol, Other Drugs and Gambling Awareness and Prevention, and Butt Out. Go to: To find out how to contact your local office for more information look up the address in this endnote.[40]

Denise Hargroves, a mental health promotion and wellness instructor, at CFB Kingston, gives us some examples of what courses and programs are available to CF members and how effective they have been. Specific personal examples are as follows.

A major addresses his squadron prior to a mental health promotion briefing by telling his members that the Chain of Command fully supports any of them registering for the *Stress: Take Charge!* and disclosing that he has taken and benefited from the course himself.

A Sergeant introduces the guest speaker for a *Suicide Awareness* briefing and encourages everyone to pay close attention to this vitally important subject by disclosing that his son had thoughts of suicide.

When a CO is made aware that one of his subordinates is being harassed by his superiors for having taken the *Managing Angry Moments* course, he brings the issue up at his next O group (Orders Group) and makes it clear that this will not be tolerated, and that the Chain of Command (C of C) will ensure that members are encouraged and supported when seeking this type of professional development.

A Unit CO who participated in the *Basic Relationship Training Course* with his spouse noted "We recognized with hope that these tools will help us to build on what we have to work through, what previously was perceived as insurmountable issues." He went on to enthusiastically promote the course with his subordinates and his peers.[41]

These leaders understand that CF members' mental and social health is every bit as important as their physical fitness to operational readiness, as well as to overall health and wellbeing. They understand that their subordinates respect leaders who see them as whole people, not automatons, and who support them in being proactive about their health and wellness.

7.1.3. Stigma

Stigma is defined as a mark or stain or reproach on one's reputation. It can also be a defect or disease like the scaly stigmata of leprosy. Throughout the ages, lepers have been feared, shunned and isolated as unclean, forced into colonies away from the general population where until recently they have been left to slowly decay as their digits and limbs rot off from oozing pestilent bacterial infection. With newly developed antibiotics many are now recovering from this dreaded disease. But it remains with us. The same sort of stigma is still attached to mental health issues.

General Rick Hillier, CDS for over three years from 2005 to 2008, said that "not all wounds are visible, and the invisible wounds of mental illness are no less real, challenging, or potentially life threatening. In fact, sometimes they are more so." Suicides in the CF are almost universally due to mental illness challenges.

Stigma is a mark of disgrace; it can be a brand, stain, blemish, defect, a scar or mark of shame or discredit. We are uncomfortable and fearful about mental illness and stigmatize those who have it. We are blissfully unaware of how many mentally ill people we encounter every day. There are many; it is the invisible illness. Stigma is disrespectful, promotes negative stereotypes, and is judgmental. It marks those suffering with mental illness as weak and dangerous. Some of the less informed even think it's contagious. Stigma has been proven as a barrier to recovery, and to many living with stigma, is worse than the illness itself.

7.1.4. Myths About Mental Illness

There are numerous myths about OSIs, and these myths are a big part of what stops afflicted soldiers from seeking help.

Myth - they feel they will be considered weak.

Reality - mental illness can affect anyone at any time.

Myth - they will be released from the CF.

Reality - 70% who seek early help go back to work.

Myth - there is an identifiable cause.

Reality - OSIs are caused by a combination of factors.

Myth - stress injuries are different than physical injuries.

Reality - OSIs are just as legitimate and just as serious as physical injuries.

Myth - OSI suffers fake their injuries.

Reality - It is very difficult to fake these symptoms. Given the stigma, why would anyone pretend that they had an OSI?

Myth - Peers, leaders and family members will think less of a member asking for help.

Reality - It takes real courage to ask for help.

What are the barriers to a soldier seeking Mental Health (MH) Services? Soldiers realize that they will most likely be seen as weak and treated differently. Their peers may be less confident in their competence. Leaders could blame them for their illness and it could well harm their career. To a field soldier it can be too embarrassing, and many don't trust mental health professionals. Furthermore, what are the main reasons for not seeking help? The main reasons are mistrust of the military hierarchy along with time barriers, resource barriers, and perhaps most damaging, to seeking help, fear of stigma.

7.2. The Leader's Role

What can we as leaders do to help reduce and mitigate these myths, barriers and perceptions for not seeking help? First, we can educate ourselves and our subordinates by carefully reading this essay and disseminating the information. Specifically, we must educate ourselves and our subordinates about OSIs to recognize symptoms and take appropriate action. We must reduce job related barriers and know available resources and information available for mitigating OSIs and helping those afflicted. We need to monitor and reduce stigma by minimizing rumours. We must foster a healthy work environment by promoting wellness and watch for behavioural changes. And, probably most importantly, we are required to lead by example while building cohesion and teamwork.

8.0. Conclusion

In future conflicts all electronic technology may be unworkable due to jamming, EMP (Electro Magnetic Pulse) or other nefarious means of interference. We may be forced to use first principle methods described above without wireless or computer communications. Normally modern forces that join in serious combat are fairly evenly matched in weapons, equipment and combat training. Leaders are probably also evenly matched, and both sides of the conflict are confident that they will win (or they probably wouldn't have joined battle in the first place). Military training regimens of First World countries around the world are similar and produce similarly effective soldiers; weapons and equipment are much alike in both utility and effectiveness. If all the measures listed above regarding command and control and the Principles of War and the Principles of Leadership are adhered to by the belligerents, there will be little to differentiate them. All things being equal the advantage will be with the force with the best morale.

Leaders in the CF must work hard to ensure that we have that advantage by maintaining high morale in their command and gaining the trust of all troops by ensuring and demonstrating professional competence. Understanding stress, crisis and fear and their effects on human nature along with the many symptoms and warning signs of OSIs is key to maintaining good morale and mitigating the effects of OSIs that may be developing. Knowing how to administer Mental Health First Aid to effect strong cohesiveness, resilience and teamwork and as a protective mechanism. This will help to develop camaraderie and inclusiveness for the soldiers who engage in combat. This brings soldiers closer together in an atmosphere of shared suffering,

More pedestrian things that irritate soldiers normally include the system, the hierarchy (all ranks with authority over the private soldier), from lance corporal, unpaid, through the non-commissioned officer (NCO) rank and all up through the officer ranks from second lieutenant to Colonels and Generals. Other irritants are: pedantic and confusing rules and regulations, the weather, and 'chicken shit" discipline often administered by the vaunted military police or self-important superiors.

Things that scare soldiers include bombardment along with the loud noises that accompanies shelling; enemy attacks and the vagaries of combat that breeds chaos and confusion, injury and death with the attendant stress and anxiety that comes with it. Things that hurt and kill them are, barbed wire, mines, booby traps, artillery and machine gun fire and snipers, and enemy attacks both ground and air and naval bombardment. Also, recently included in the mix are improvised explosive devices (IEDs) and RPGs (rocket propelled grenades) supplied in numbers by the Russians and Chinese, which have plagued our soldiers fighting terrorist groups.

Leaders must keep these things in mind and watch carefully for signs of crisis, fear, and stress; along with stigma, to mitigate their effects before an OSI develops in their soldiers or worse in themselves.

It is our solemn duty as leaders in the CF.

Endnotes

---

[1] Mental Health First Aid Veteran Community, Mental Health Commission of Canada; Veterans Affairs Canada, 2016.

[2] Charles R. Figley and William P. Nash, Combat Stress Injury, Theory, Research and Management; Routledge Taylor and Francis Group, 270 Madison Avenue, New York, 2007.p. xv.

[3] English, John A., *On Infantry*. New York, Praeger Publishers, 1981. P.206, NOTES.

[4] Mimms, John A., Spam Medal Heroes, Barrie ON, Video Text Inc., 1984, p.63.

[5] Leadership in the Canadian Forces: Leading People, Canadian Defence Academy - Canadian Forces Leadership Institute; Her Majesty the Queen in right of Canada2007.

[6] Funk and Wagnalls Canadian College Dictionary; Funk and Wagnalls Publishing Company, INC. Markham Ontario, 1986.

[7] Tricycle, The Buddhist Review, edited by James Shaheen, Lane Press, Burlington, VT, U.S.A., Fall 2017.
[8] Hadassah Review Vol 99, No 2, American Jewish Press Association Magazine Publishers of America, November/December 2017, p
[9] Tricycle, The Buddhist Review, edited by James Shaheen, Lane Press, Burlington, VT, U.S.A., Fall 2017
[10] Presentation, Dennis K. at AA meeting April 2018; Verona Ontario.
[11] Ibid.
[12] Daniel Wegner, Harvard Psychologist,
[13] Thompson, J.M. et all, Mental Health of Canadian Armed Forces Veterans - review of population studies. Journal of Military Veterans and Family Health, Vol1, No. 2; 2016.
[14] Roy-Byrne, P.P., Stang, P. Wittchen, H.U. et al. (2000) lifetime panic-depression co-morbidity in National Co-morbidity study. Association with symptoms, impairment. Course and help seeking. British Journal of Psychiatry.
[15] American Psychiatric Association. (2013) Diagnostic and statistical manual of mental disorders; DSM 5. Washington D. C. American Psychiatric association.
[16] Shelbourne, C.D., Wells, K.B. and Judd, L.L. (1996) Functioning and wellbeing of patients with panic disorder, American Journal of Psychiatry.
[17] Weissman, M. Klerman, G., Markowitz, J. & Ouellette, R. (1989) Suicidal ideation and suicide attempts in panic disorders and attacks., New England Journal of Medicine, p.22.
[18] Ibid, p.32.
[19] Ibid p.34.
[20] Ibid.
[21] Ibid.
[22] Shelbourne, C.D., Wells, K.B. and Judd, L.L. (1996) Functioning and wellbeing of patients with panic disorder, American Journal of Psychiatry, 153, pp. 213.
[23] Shelbourne, C.D., Wells, K.B. and Judd, L.L. (1996) Functioning and wellbeing of patients with panic disorder, American Journal of Psychiatry, 153, pp. 213.
[24] Weissman, M. Klerman, G., Markowitz, J. & Ouellette, R. (1989) Suicidal ideation and suicide attempts in panic disorders and attacks., New England Journal of Medicine,
[25] Ibid. P.22.
[26] Ibid. P.29.
[27] Ibid.
[28] Sermon by Chaplain General. National War Memorial, 11 Nov 2017.
[29] Leaders and suicide prevention, Mental Health First Aid, Veterans Community, Veterans Affairs Canada; Mental Health Commission of Canada, 2016.
[30] Crisis First Aid by Leaders

[31] Leadership in the Canadian Forces: Leading People, Canadian Defence Academy - Canadian Forces Leadership Institute; Her Majesty the Queen in right of Canada2007, P.iii.
[32] Ibid. P.
[33] Interview by author with Major General, Colonel of the Regiment, RCR, July 1973.
[34] English, John A., *On Infantry*. New York, Praeger Publishers, 1981.
[35] Canadian Army Manual of Training (CAMT) 7 - 45, Infantry Section leading and Platoon Tactics; War Office Publication, School of Infantry, Canadian Forces headquarters, Ottawa, 1954.
[36] Ibid. P.
[37] Petronius Arbiter, General, Roman Legion.
[38] Leadership in the Canadian Forces: Leading People, Canadian Defence Academy - Canadian Forces Leadership Institute; Her Majesty the Queen in right of Canada2007, p. 9.
[39] Ibid, p. 61.
[40] http://www.forces.gc.ca/health-sante/ps/hpp-pps/links-liens-eng.asp
[41] OSISS History by W.A. Leavey 2009, Unpublished.

Appendix A

MORAL INJURY

Also included in the mix is morale injury which is when a soldier's moral values and ethical and humanitarian sensibilities are violated. Morale injury is best illustrated by an example:

An Airborne trooper describes his tour in Somalia. "The Peacekeepers role was hard" he said "The rules of engagement (ROE) were very ambiguous. They were changing daily. It's okay, we can't kill the guy today, but tomorrow we're going to change. Then the next day, if he's carrying a weapon you can shoot him, but today you can't. It was utterly ridiculous."

The Trooper describes a situation where he finds himself struggling with the ROE.

A Somali man comes to the front gate hollering screaming and swinging a machete while hacking away at the gate. The soldier peacekeepers, with their weapons up tell him to drop the machete. One fires a few warning shots overhead. The man is ready to throw the machete.

The trooper is thinking of the ROE, "I can't shoot him in the thigh or I'll go to jail, "I can't shoot him there or I'll go to jail. If I shoot him here I'll go to jail. I just worked my way down and ended up shooting him in the ankle. He still didn't stop. He still didn't drop it. I put two more rounds in his foot. It was about another minute and a half. He was still hopping around."

About a week later the trooper was admitted to the hospital with the dreaded Mogadishu virus. They ended up bringing the Somali in too. "They kept us separate, but it was traumatizing just the same… they brought him in because I guess he was getting infection," and "They didn't want him dying. So, they dressed his wound and sent him home."

"I think about it a lot, I wonder if he died from infection. Sometimes I wonder if I was in the right or not. I could have killed the guy. I still would have been right. Inevitably, I think he would have released the machete. Sometimes I deal with it and wonder if he's alive."

The ambiguity of the ROE delayed the trooper's decision for a minute and a half which could have cost his or one of his mate's serious injury or even death.

Because of ambiguous ROE, it is more important to decide what part of a man's body to shoot rather than react quickly in order to protect his or his brother soldier's bodies. The trooper decides to shoot the man in the ankle and foot as the least likely to result in jail time. When the Somali was brought to the hospital he was afraid that the man would try to attack him. If this was to happen, ironically, the trooper would have to struggle with the ROE again. (Can I choke him out or must I just restrain him).

To this day, the trooper questions his decision to shoot the Somali. He wonders if he did the right thing and if the man is still alive. He has suffered a moral injury.

Appendix B

HOLMES-RAHE STRESS EVALUATION

- **Add together the point values of the events that have occurred in your life in the past year.**
    - Death of a spouse...100
    - Marital separation...65
    - Death of a close family member...63
    - Personal injury or illness... 63
    - Marriage...50
    - Loss of job...47
    - Marital reconciliation...45
    - Retirement...45
    - Change in health of a family member...44
    - Pregnancy...40
    - Sex difficulties... 39
    - Gain of a mew family member...39
    - Change in financial status...38
    - Death of a close friend...37
    - Change to a different kind of work...36
    - Increase or decrease in arguments with spouse...35
    - Taking out a big mortgage on a home...31
    - Foreclosure of mortgage or loan...30
    - Change in work responsibilities...30
    - Son or daughter leaving home...29
    - Trouble with in-laws...29
    - Outstanding personal achievement...28
    - Spouse beginning or stopping work...29
    - Revision of personal habits...24
    - Trouble with business superior...23
    - Change in work hours or conditions...20
    - Change in residence...20
    - Change in schools...20
    - Change in recreation...19

- Change in social activities...l8
- Taking out a small mortgage on your home...17
- Change in sleeping habits...16
- Change in number of family get-togethers...15
- Change in eating habits...15
- Vacation...13
- Minor violations of law...11

Appendix C

PHYSICAL STRESS WARNING SIGNS

- Backaches and stiffness in neck;
- Difficulty breathing;
- Dryness of the throat and mouth;
- Weakness or dizziness;
- Chest pains and tightness in the chest;
- Frequent colds and coughing;
- Persistent diarrhea
- Flushed (reddish) complexion due to high blood pressure;
- Headaches, including migraine;
- Cold hands or feet;
- Excessive perspiration;
- Frequent urination;
- Indigestion;
- Vomiting;
- Premenstrual tension or missed menstrual cycles;
- Insomnia;
- Heart palpitations;
- Skin ailments such as acne and rashes;
- Frequent tiredness;
- Slow recovery from illness or surgery;
- Bruxism, or grinding of the teeth; and
- Trembling, nervous tics.

Appendix D

GOLDBERG ANXIETY SCALE

The Goldberg Anxiety Scale is and internationally known scale for screening anxiety. In it you score one point for each 'Yes" if the symptom occurs most of the time over the previous 2 - 4 weeks. The questions include:

- Have you felt keyed up, on edge?
- Have you been worrying a lot?
- Have you been irritable?
- Have you had difficulty relaxing? (If 'Yes" to two of the above, go on to e - i.
- Have you been sleeping poorly?
- Have you had headaches or neck aches?
- Have you had trembling, tingling, dizzy spells, sweating, urinary frequency, or diarrhea?
- Have you been worried about your health?
- Have you had difficulty sleeping?

Appendix E

FITNESS AND LIFESTYLE EVALUATION IN THE CF

CF Programs are:
Fitness testing (EXPRESS,
MSR, STEP,
Basic Military Swimming Standard Test,
LFCPFS) Battle space.
These programs are designed to improve and maintain:

- Accountability and Responsibility
- Operational Focus
- Measurable
- Healthy Nutrition (What, when to eat)
- Daily physical activity
- Healthy Weight
- Addiction Free
- Stamina/Endurance

Nutrition - A **Strong Mind in a Strong Body** (You are what you eat). Considerations are:

- Top Fuel for Top Performance
- Major Classes of Nutrients
- Portion Sizes
- Water
- Fuel Mix
- Carbohydrates
- Protein
- Fat
- Minerals and Vitamins
- Timing of Food and fluid intake
- Fuel before work/activity
- Fuel during work/activity
- Fuel after work/activity
- BMI Body Composition and weight loss

- Dietary supplements
- Weight Wellness
- BMI

Sleep. As mentioned earlier, poor sleep or lack of sleep is inevitable in operations. The circadian rhythm, where light and darkness influences the sleep cycle also has an effect. As well, soldiers are almost constantly fatigued in battle due to consistent anxiety, arduous activity, weather and noise. Fatigue will slow down mental processes which makes it even more vital to use battle procedure and orders formats learned and practiced by all ranks. As leaders, it is our job to know the effects of sleep deprivation and organize our soldiers as a team and employ them up to their capabilities.[1] Tasks must be allocated equitably, shifts must be established to allow at least half of the unit to rest at a time when not in contact with the enemy. Things to watch and plan for are:

- Routine
- Caffeine
- Alcohol
- Biofeedback
- Circadian Rhythm
- Stress hormones,
- Yoga,
- Concentration
- Problem Solving
- Tai chi
- Memory
- Antibodies
- Sleep apnea
- Smoking
- Insomnia
- Depression

Safety. Another factor in wellness that is often overlooked is safety. Factors to be considered are:

- Safety Equipment;
- Fire Safety;

- Seat Belts;
- Vehicle Maintenance;
- WHMIS;
- Traffic;
- Cold weather;
- Hot Weather;
- Communicable Disease;
- Medication;
- Water;
- Electric Shock;
- Burns.

Endnotes

---

[1] The Principles of Leadership.CFP131(!) para 405.

About Lammi Publishing Inc.

Incorporated in 2014, Lammi Publishing is dedicated to publishing Canadian military history from the wars before confederation to the mission in Afghanistan. Our philosophy is that we cannot forget. Our mission is to be a method of remembrance. Canadian military history has shaped not only our politics and government, but our society as well. Canadians naturally take pride in our famous victories in Western Europe, Afghanistan and South Africa. From the oceans to the air, Canadians have done their duty with skill and valor. Peacekeeping operations have taken our forces far and wide bringing hope and security to so many. Canadian uniforms have been seen around the world as harbingers of liberation, from Belgium in WWI to the Netherlands in WWII to Yugoslavia in the 1990's.

It is only by having easy access to material on these events that we can understand them, put them in context and remember. Information, analysis, and the memoires of those who served should be readily available instead of being locked away in a desk or a long forgotten bookcase in the back of a library.

The rise of electronic books means that it is now possible for anyone to easily compile a library that would rival the best that our public libraries or universities can offer, with no more worries about short print runs and the vagaries of the antiquarian market.

To learn more about us and what we are doing, check out our website: http://lammipublishing.ca

Lammi
Publishing Inc.

CPSIA information can be obtained
at www.ICGtesting.com
Printed in the USA
LVHW082329170422
716440LV00014BA/1033

9 781988 932057